HOKUSAI

One Hundred Views of Mt. Fuji

HOKUSAI

One Hundred Views of Mt. Fuji

INTRODUCTION AND COMMENTARIES

ON THE PLATES BY

HENRY D. SMITH II

GEORGE BRAZILLER, INC., PUBLISHERS

NEW YORK

Published in 1988 by George Braziller, Inc.

Reproduced from the illustrated book *Fugaku Hyakkei* by Hokusai in the Spencer Collection, Sorimachi 579, New York Public Library Astor, Lenox and Tilden Foundation.

Introduction and commentaries on the plates © George Braziller, Inc. 1988.

For information address the publisher:

George Braziller, Inc.
60 Madison Avenue
New York, New York 10010

Library of Congress Cataloging-in-Publication Data

Katsushika, Hokusai, 1760–1849.
  One hundred views of Mt. Fuji.

  Original running title: Fugaku hyakkei.
  Includes bibliography.
  1. Katsushika, Hokusai, 1760–1849—Themes, motives.   2. Fuji, Mount (Japan) in art.   I. Smith, Henry DeWitt.   II. Title.   III. Title: 100 views of Mt. Fuji.   IV. Title: Fugaku hyakkei.
NE1325.K3A4   1988   769.92'4   87-36827
ISBN 0-8076-1195-6

First Edition.

Designed by Gerald Pryor.
Printed and bound in Japan by Toppan Printing Company.
Photography by Phillip Pocock.

ACKNOWLEDGMENTS

I am indebted above all to Suzuki Jūzō, both for his own published commentaries on the *One Hundred Views of Mt. Fuji*, on which I have drawn heavily, and for personal conversations about Hokusai. Roger Keyes has shared with me his library and his considerable expertise on Hokusai, of whose prints he and Peter Morse are now preparing a *catalogue raisonné*. Haruko Iwasaki of Harvard University helped with the translations of the prefaces and offered interpretive insights. Jack Hillier, whose own work has taught me much about both Hokusai and the Japanese illustrated book, kindly lent me a copy of Frederick Dickins's original commentaries of 1880. Finally, I would like to dedicate this effort to the memory of my father-in-law, Dr. Kondō Shunshirō, who like Hokusai offered me many precious lessons about growing old well.

CONTENTS

✌ Introduction ✌
Hokusai and the Mountain of Immortality

One Hundred Views of Mt. Fuji is a work of such unending visual delight that it is easy to overlook its underlying spiritual intent. Hokusai was, as he prefaced his signature, "Seventy-five Years of Age" when the first volume of the work appeared in 1834, and his effort to capture the great mountain from every angle, in every context, was in the deepest sense a prayer for the gift of immortality that lay hidden within the heart of the volcano. By showing life itself in all its shifting forms against the unchanging form of Fuji, with the vitality and wit that inform every page of the book, he sought not only to prolong his own life but in the end to gain admission to the realm of the Immortals.

Signaling this quest, Hokusai announced in the signature a change of name, the fifth and last such change that he would make in the course of his long career.[1] He was no longer "Iitsu, Formerly Hokusai," but now "Manji, Old Man Mad about Painting." Manji is "the figure of ten thousand," the ancient religious symbol of the swastika, giver of life and fortune. The signature was followed by this famous declaration:

> From the age of six I had a penchant for copying the form of things, and from
> about fifty, my pictures were frequently published; but until the age of seventy,
> nothing that I drew was worthy of notice. At seventy-three years, I was
> somewhat able to fathom the growth of plants and trees, and the structure of
> birds, animals, insects, and fish. Thus when I reach eighty years, I hope to
> have made increasing progress, and at ninety to see further into the underlying
> principles of things, so that at one hundred years I will have achieved a divine
> state in my art, and at one hundred and ten, every dot and every stroke will be
> as though alive. Those of you who live long enough, bear witness that these
> words of mine prove not false.
>
> Told by Gakyō Rōjin Manji

The inner meaning of these lines will be explored further, but it should be clear that Hokusai felt himself, at the age of seventy-five, to be making a new personal break-through with the *One Hundred Views of Mt. Fuji*. Modern critics and connoisseurs have tended to second Hokusai's intentions, if inadvertently, in the widespread judgment that this work is Hokusai's masterpiece. But it is in fact less well known than the *Thirty-Six Views of Mt. Fuji* which immediately preceded it, the famous set of forty-six prints (ten more than promised) that marked the beginning of Hokusai's courtship of the mountain. The reason is simple: the *Thirty-Six Views* are large single-sheet color prints, while the *One Hundred Views* is a book, in three small volumes, printed in monochrome black and gray. It is also a work that achieves true masterpiece status only in the original edition, which is reproduced here, but which has been known largely through later states with clumsy printing from worn.

The organization of the *One Hundred Views of Mt. Fuji* in book form is particu-larly important, for it provides a totality and an order of presentation that is absent in the single-sheet series. For Western viewers, it takes practice to accustom the eye to Japanese style: reading from right to left. It will soon become apparent, however, that the compositions were intended to be seen in this way: note for example that the position of Mt. Fuji itself tends on the average to be right of center; and in those compositions in which the mountain assumes an assertive role in the overall design, it will almost always be on the right. The actual order of the views seems to have a secret inner logic, offering sequences that both please and perplex, enhancing the experience of viewing the work as a whole.

To reach the inner meanings of the *One Hundred Views of Mt. Fuji*, however, it is necessary to know something of the mountain and its place in Hokusai's culture.

The Peerless Peak

In the upper left or right corner of each of the 102 separate views in the *One Hundred Views of Mt. Fuji* appears a title, which usually contains the name "Fuji" written with the characters "not-two" (*fu-ni*), that is, having no equal: peerless. As with so many Japanese place names, this is a "folk etymology" of a word whose true origins can only be surmised. (One frequently mentioned candidate is *huchi*, the Ainu word for "fire god," but this is by no means definite.)[2] "Peerless" is not the most common way of writing Fuji, either in Hokusai's time or today, which rather uses the characters "prosperous gentleman" (itself a folk etymology). Hokusai uses this more familiar combination only once, and then for a special reason (No. 31).

Hokusai's orthographic insistence on the "peerless" quality of Fuji nevertheless taps the most basic Japanese understanding of this very special mountain. This begins with the fact that Mt. Fuji *is* peerless. At 12,385 feet, it is by far the highest mountain in Japan, almost twenty percent above its nearest rivals. It is also a volcano and was frequently active throughout most of Japanese history, particularly in the eighth and ninth centuries when the dominant legends were taking shape. Fuji today is so tame (although still technically classified as active) that we tend to see it as a passive symbol. Not so for Hokusai, however, for whom the last great eruption in 1707, which left the Hōeizan crater on the southeast slope (see Nos. 7–8), would have been within living memory at the time of his birth in 1760.

In modern times, Fuji has become so much the tool of chauvinists and commercial image-makers that it has degenerated into a hackneyed and passive symbol for Japan itself. In earlier times, however, the national pride invested in Fuji seemed more naive and passionate. From an early point, Fuji was envisioned as peerless not only within Japan, but within the entire known world. "Sangoku ichi," it was called, "First among the Three Countries"—of India, China, and Japan. This belief was reflected in legends about Chinese coming to pay homage to the mountain (as in the Nō drama *Fujisan*), and in reports of the fame and even visibility of Fuji from very distant places on the Asian mainland (see No. 73).

The latent nationalism of Mt. Fuji became increasingly explicit in the course of the Tokugawa period, through the nativist revival known as National Learning (Kokugaku).

This led to an escalation during the later Tokugawa period in the production of poetry and art celebrating Mt. Fuji, creating both precedents for Hokusai (particularly, as we shall see, in the genre of "one hundred Fujis") and a generally favorable climate for new and different ways of depicting the mountain. The overt tone of celebration that runs throughout the *One Hundred Views of Mt. Fuji* played to this undercurrent of national pride.

The Sacred Peak

Hokusai's own deeper concerns, however, had little to do with Fuji as symbol of Japan: his was rather an essentially religious preoccupation, a concern with life and death. Religious faith in Fuji stemmed from the primitive Japanese veneration of all mountains as sacred and is reflected in Hokusai's opening depiction of the mountain as a Shintō goddess. As an organized religion, however, the worship of Fuji evolved primarily within the context of Buddhism, among the wandering mountain ascetics who came to be known as *yamabushi*.[3] Their semilegendary patron saint, En no Gyōja, is depicted by Hokusai in No. 3 of the *One Hundred Views of Mt. Fuji*, fearlessly practicing nighttime austerities on the summit of Fuji during his exile in Oshima in the late seventh century.

In fact, however, no mortal would have seriously considered climbing Fuji in such early times, since it was a very active volcano, with as many as fifteen eruptions between 781 and 1083.[4] It was not until the year 1149, precisely in the era when *yamabushi* practice was taking the form of the coherent religious cult known as Shugendō, that we have a credible record of the human ascent of Fuji, by a holy man named Matsudai. By the sixteenth century, the Shugendō center located at Murayama on the southern skirts of Mt. Fuji had expanded beyond the practice of professional priests to become the gateway for climbing by lay believers as well.

With the shift of the political center of gravity eastward following the establishment of the Tokugawa shogunate in 1603, so also the orientation of Fuji worship changed. Before that time, Fuji had been both worshipped and perceived largely from the direction of the imperial capital of Kyoto, along the Tokaido highway that approached Fuji from the southwest. Thus Yamabe Akahito's poem, which Hokusai illustrates in No. 57, envisions Fuji from Tago to the south, and the standard view of Fuji in painting was over the pines of Miho in the same direction. But then for political reasons, the Shugendō complex at Murayama declined sharply in power in the seventeenth century, and in precisely the same period there emerged a new cult which worshipped Fuji from a different direction, that of Edo by way of the gateway at Yoshida on the northern side of the peak.

This new Edo religion of Fuji was known simply as Fujikō, after the local confraternities (*kō*) into which it was organized. Its founder was an ascetic named Kakugyō (1541–1646, dates which may reflect Fuji's association with longevity more than his actual lifespan), to whom En no Gyōja appeared in a vision, instructing him to climb the mountain from the north, or "front" (*omote*)—an explicit rejection of the Shugendō tradition to the south as the "back." Throughout the course of the Edo period, the Fujikō grew as a popular religion and was given a particular boost when one of its leaders, Jikigyō Miroku, died on the mountain in the year 1733 after a self-imposed fast of thirty-one days. Followers of the Fujikō understood the deity of Mt. Fuji, whom they called Sengen Daibosatsu, to be a transcendental god, and their belief placed an emphasis on everyday morality that set it apart from the more magical practices of medieval Shugendō.

It has often been suggested that the popularity of the Fujikō cult was an important element in Hokusai's decision to undertake his two series depicting Mt. Fuji.[5] It is certainly true that the Fujikō was widely popular by the early nineteenth century among Edo commoners, many of whom made annual pilgrimages to the summit of Fuji by the Yoshida route. For those unable to make the climb—particularly women, who by lingering Shugendō tradition were forbidden to ascend sacred peaks—the Fujikō believers began in 1779 to construct miniature replicas of Fuji within the city of Edo. By ascending one of the mini-Fuji mounds, which were about ten-to-twenty-feet high, it was believed that one would achieve the same merit afforded by climbing the real peak. By the time that Hokusai's *Thirty-Six Views of Mt. Fuji* began to appear, ten of these miniature mountains had been built in Edo.

It is doubtful, however, that Hokusai had any detailed knowledge of the Fujikō or its practices. He was himself a devout believer in the Nichiren sect of Buddhism, particularly in the cult of the Boddhisattva Myōken, the personification of the Big Dipper (hence, at least two of his various names, Hokusai and Taito, refer to the North Star around which the Dipper revolves); and it is highly unlikely that this allegiance would have allowed for any particular interest in the Fujikō. He clearly had some idea of Fujikō climbing practices, for he depicted them in four separate views (Nos. 5, 6, 46, and 76). All of these are highly fanciful, however, and it is doubtful that Hokusai had ever been able to observe the Fujikō pilgrims closely, much less to climb the mountain himself. Their depiction is surely a reflection of the widespread popularity of the Fujikō in Edo, but this popularity itself was probably only a minor factor in Hokusai's decision to focus on the mountain.

The Deathless Peak

Hokusai's spiritual preoccupation with Fuji is thus not to be found in the organized worship of the mountain but rather in a different tradition, one which is Taoist rather than Buddhist in origin: the belief in Fuji as the source of the secret of immortality. Although he wrote "Fuji" with the characters meaning "not-two," his real intentions are to be found in still another folk etymology of Fuji as "not-death" (*fu-shi*), hence immortal.

The classical source for this etymology is the conclusion to "The Tale of the Bamboo Cutter" (Taketori monogatari), a story of about the ninth century.[6] There, a heavenly maiden returns to the sky after a sojourn on earth during which she won the heart of the emperor, to whom she left a letter and a jar containing the elixir of immortality. The distraught emperor ordered these to be taken to the summit of a great volcano in Suruga Province and there committed to the flames. From that time, the story concludes, smoke continued to rise from the peak, which was given the name "Fuji," or "not-death."

The conception of Fuji as deathless was carried on in the medieval Nō play *Fujisan*, in which an envoy of the Chinese emperor is shown arriving in Japan in the hopes of finding the famed medicine of immortality. The envoy notes that a Taoist practitioner from China had earlier traveled to Fuji in search of the elixir. This is a reference to a report in the Chinese *Chronicles of History* (Shih Chi) that the Ch'in emperor in the third century B.C. had sent a Taoist adept named Hsü Fu (in Japanese, Jofuku) to seek out the Three Mountains of the Immortals and bring back the magic elixir. As the legend was handed down among the Japanese, one of the magic mountains was Fuji. In the Nō play, the Chinese envoy's wish is granted when Sengen Daibosatsu, the Buddhist deity of Fuji, appears in the form of Kaguya Hime, the heavenly maiden of "The Tale of the Bamboo Cutter," and grants some of the elixir.

Thus from an early time, Mt. Fuji was seen as the source of the secret of immortality, a tradition that was at the heart of Hokusai's own obsession with the mountain. Although none of Hokusai's views specifically depict this tradition, it is in effect his hidden agenda. Proof that others understood this is to be found in the preface to the third and last volume of the *One Hundred Views of Mt. Fuji*, where the author speculates that Hokusai at the age of ninety had indeed discovered the famed elixir on the summit of the mountain.

Hokusai at Seventy-three

Hokusai was a late-bloomer. He entered the profession of print-making at the early age of fourteen, as a carver's apprentice, and soon moved into designing as a student of Shunshō. The details of his career have often been told and need not be repeated here save to emphasize that he was continually changing, experimenting with different styles and shifting between the media of single-sheet color prints, privately published prints (*surimono*), picture books, instruction manuals for drawing, and illustrations for popular fiction. It was particularly the latter two categories that gained him a wide popular following in his fifties and sixties. But it was to be his work of his seventies, led by *Thirty-Six Views of Mt. Fuji* and climaxed by the *One Hundred Views*, which would win him his most lasting fame.

In earlier landscape work both in single-sheet prints and in books, Hokusai had often shown Fuji, but with no greater interest than any other artist. The first sign of some particular attachment came in a design manual of 1823 entitled *Contemporary Patterns for Combs and Pipes* (Imayō sekkin hinagata).[7] Included among the designs was a set of eight views of Fuji surmounting the shape of a comb, some of which suggest precedents for the later Fuji series (see for example No. 33). A publisher's advertisement at the end of the same book lists *Eight Forms of Fuji* (Fuji hattai) as a forthcoming work by Hokusai that would show "landscapes as they differ according to the movements of the heavens, in clear skies, under rain, wind, snow, and mist, through the four seasons."[8] No such work was ever issued, but it hints at the beginning of an interest in capturing Fuji in a variety of guises.

Meanwhile, Hokusai was advancing in years, having in 1821 reached the important age of 61 (by Japanese count, which includes the year of birth and advances one year each New Year's Day), when one returns to the year in the sexagenary cycle in which one began. Even before this, Hokusai had already revealed his intense preoccupation with aging when he signed himself "Old Man" (Rōjin) as early as age 46.[9] And yet it was not until just about the time he turned seventy that his lust for longer life and his preoccupation with Fuji were finally brought together in the *Thirty-Six Views of Mt. Fuji*.[10]

It is crucial at this point to refer back to the postscript to the *One Hundred Views of Mt. Fuji* that was quoted at the beginning of this essay. This celebrated statement is, in its overall pattern, a parody of the familiar lines from the "Analects" (2:4).[11]

> At fifteen, I set my heart on learning. At thirty, I was firmly established. At forty, I had no more doubts. At fifty, I knew the will of Heaven. At sixty, I was ready to listen to it. At seventy, I could follow my heart's desire without transgressing what was right.

Hokusai, however, takes up where Confucius left off, by beginning at age seventy and proceeding for four more decades to the age of one hundred ten. The first sign of the preoccupation that sets Hokusai apart from Confucius is to be found in the use of the term "half-hundred" (*hanpyaku*) to refer to the age of "fifty."

Hokusai next asserts that he produced nothing of worth before the age of seventy, thereby implying that only at that particular age did he embark on a truly worthwhile project. As it happens, it was probably shortly after reaching seventy, in the year 1829, that Hokusai took up the *Thirty-Six Views of Mt. Fuji*. The next stage is even more intriguing, however, for Hokusai specifies the age of seventy-three as the point at which he finally began to make some progress. Why this odd number of seventy-three? Something of special importance must have occurred in Hokusai's inner life in this year, the year 1832. We can only guess, but I would conjecture that it was in this year that Hokusai, having completed his designs for the *Thirty-Six Views of Mt. Fuji*, began work on the *One Hundred Views*.

Various writers have speculated over the years as to Hokusai's motives in producing the *One Hundred Views of Mt. Fuji*, but the waters have been muddied by the implausible theory that he was driven by a sense of rivalry with the much younger Hiroshige, whose famous *Fifty-Three Stages of the Tōkaidō* appeared between late 1832 and early 1834. This theory was elaborated by Narazaki Muneshige in his *Hokusai ron* of 1944, in which he fantasized at length about Hokusai's envy at the sudden success of Hiroshige, concluding that the old artist decided to respond with the *One Hundred Views of Mt. Fuji*.[12]

Implausible as it was, Narazaki's fanciful explanation, in time, found its way into every corner of the literature on Hokusai, where it remained virtually unchallenged until at last laid to rest in the early 1970s by Nagata Seiji and Suzuki Jūzō.[13] The theory, which is lacking in any direct evidence, simply defies common sense. To begin with, the timing is wrong since Hokusai must have begun the *One Hundred Views* before Hiroshige's Tōkaidō series had won any widespread acclaim. One also wonders why Hokusai would have responded to a set of large color prints with a small monochrome book, and why the response should have been so lacking in the lyrical sentiment that was the obvious key to Hiroshige's success.

More fundamentally, the Hiroshige-envy theory makes no sense because of Hokusai's aloof personality and has in the end done a considerable disservice by distracting attention from the introspective and ultimately spiritual qualities of the *One Hundred Views of Mt. Fuji*. This is not to deny that more mundane considerations were involved. I doubt Kojima Usui's suggestion that Hokusai simply had a lot of leftover designs from the *Thirty-Six Views*, since the format and style of design are totally different.[14] More plausible is Suzuki Jūzō's proposal that the popularity of the *Thirty-Six Views* created a demand for what would today amount to a paperback edition—an economical version that would make more designs accessible to more people. But this fails to explain why such particular care went into the design and printing of the book.

In the end, I am convinced that the *One Hundred Views of Mt. Fuji* was conceived as a totally new and particularly special work for Hokusai. The continuity with the *Thirty-Six Views* is undeniable, for it appears strongly in a number of related designs (see in particular Nos. 4, 13, 33, 40, 46, 52, 53, 57, 97). But some such continuity is inevitable in view of the lack of almost any interval between the two series, and in all such instances of parallel theme, the differences are even more revealing than the similarities. To understand the true inner dynamics of the *One Hundred Views*, we must probe more deeply into the psyche of the aging artist.

One Hundred Fujis

Why one hundred views of Fuji? The simple answer is that, by the 1830s, enough artists and poets had already done some sort of "one hundred Fujis" that it had become a genre in its own right. The oldest precedents were poetic, dating back to at least the early seventeenth century, when Minase Ujinari composed one hundred waka on Fuji.[15] Much better known and more accessible was the work that is mentioned at the beginning of Ryūtei Tanehiko's introduction to the first volume of the *One Hundred Views of Mt. Fuji*. Entitled *One Hundred Waka in Praise of Mt. Fuji* (*Ei Fujisan hyakushu waka*), this was the work of Keichū (1640–1701), the Buddhist priest who laid the groundwork for the National Learning (Kokugaku) movement, and it was available in at least five printed editions between 1781 and 1836.

Tanehiko mentions one other "hundred Fujis" work in his preface, *One Hundred Haiku on Fuji by Tōchō* (*Tōchō Fuji hyakku*), a haiku collection by Wada Tōchō (1658–1706) that was published in 1692. Since only one surviving copy of this work is listed in the *Kokusho sōmokuroku* (a multivolume bibliography of premodern Japanese books and manuscripts), it was probably little known in Hokusai's time, as Tanehiko implies. But a search of the bibliography on Fuji reveals four other poetry works in the one-hundred Fuji genre that had appeared within three decades before Hokusai's work: one of haiku, one of kyōka, and two of waka. All of these were available in printed editions.[16]

It is particularly revealing that four of these seven literary precedents were not in the traditional waka form, but in the short form of haiku and the comic form of kyōka. As I argue in the legends for Nos. 60, 72, and 77, Hokusai's views offer a number of compositions that bear close structural parallels to haiku and to its comic counterpart, the senryū, of which Hokusai was himself a practitioner.

In pictorial views, the pioneer was a relatively obscure artist of Kano school lineage by the name of Kawamura Minsetsu (also Kunshaku), whose only known surviving work is a four-volume book entitled *One Hundred Fujis* (*Hyaku Fuji*), with prefaces dated 1767 (although the earliest known printed edition dates from 1771). This work seems to have been widely available and clearly had some influence on Hokusai, as Kojima Usui first suggested in 1931 and as other writers have continued to emphasize.[17] The case for direct influence, however, rests largely on two instances of compositional contrivance: one of viewing Fuji underneath a bridge (as in Nos. 48 and 85), and one through a window (as in No. 60). But Hokusai had shown Fuji seen beneath a bridge in much earlier prints, so any influence was not specific to the *Hundred Views*, and the conception of the window view, as I detail in the commentary, is very different. In my own opinion, the best instance of specific influence is to be found in the title (but not composition) of No. 49, which is identical to one from Minsetsu.

Minsetsu's more general influence on Hokusai's views of Fuji was to introduce the idea of showing Fuji from all sides rather than just from Edo or along the coast, stretching into the mountains on the "back" of Fuji and as far distant as China. Yet this influence is more relevant to the *Thirty-Six Views*, in which actual places are carefully specified much as they had been in Minsetsu's work; the *One Hundred Views* is much weaker in such specificity of place. Hence any influence of Minsetsu on Hokusai was quite general and explains little. The most revealing comment on the relationship between the two appears in the preface to the third volume of Hokusai's work, which begins by observing that "while the views of Mt. Fuji of Kunshaku [Minsetsu] are orthodox (*sei*), those of Hokusai are eccentric (*ki*)." This well captures the utter difference in the impact of the two works: on the one hand Minsetsu's sketchy and generally monotonous landscapes versus the tremendously imaginative and varied views of Hokusai.

Nor was Minsetsu the only artist before Hokusai to attempt one hundred views of Fuji. The celebrated painter Ike Taiga (1723–76) was reported, in the inscription on a memorial marker erected shortly after his death, to have painted one hundred views of Fuji, although the works themselves do not survive.[18] In the same era, probably in the mid-1770s, the ukiyo-e artist Kitao Masayoshi began a series of color prints entitled *Hyaku Fuji* (the same title as that of Minsetsu, his likely inspiration).[19] Only seven are known to have been completed, mostly views from the Tōkaidō, but Hokusai probably knew of the effort. Still more recently, the topographical artist Hasegawa Settan had executed a volume of one hundred views of Fuji in 1825, although only in manuscript and probably unknown to Hokusai.[20]

One Hundred Years

Hokusai in the end had a much more compelling reason for choosing the number one hundred than any such precedents in poetry or painting: this was the age that he was increasingly obsessed with achieving. This is clearly the deeper meaning of the colophon to Volume I, in which he claims that at the age of one hundred he will have achieved a divine state of his art. In fact, he was careful to envision himself living on past one hundred, to at least one hundred ten. The number one hundred must be understood as something more than just a specific age, although it was certainly that for Hokusai. As much as longevity, Hokusai craved immortality; he was obsessed with becoming an Immortal of Painting (*gashinsen*).[21]

Hokusai's obsession with one hundred is revealed in other parts of the colophon to Volume I of the *One Hundred Views of Mt. Fuji*, first with the new name "Manji" which he commemorated there. He had actually used this name as early as 1825, but as a writer of comic verse rather than as a painter. Only from the time of the *One Hundred Views* did it become his dominant name. The character is the sign of the swastika (from Sanskrit, "object of well-being"), the ancient religious symbol that came to Japan from India, by way of China. The symbolic origins of the swastika are obscure—one recent theory associates it with the planetary gods[22]—but in Japan it functioned generally as a magical symbol of good luck and long life, and particularly as a symbol of the Buddha. For Hokusai, however, the special significance surely lay in the literal meaning of Manji as "the symbol of ten thousand," or one hundred times one hundred.[23]

The preoccupation with one hundred carries through in an almost whimsical way to the list of "forthcoming" publications by Hokusai that concludes the colophon. These eleven titles in effect constitute a whole catalog of the world as organized by hundreds. It is doubtful that Hokusai ever actually intended to produce all these books; at any rate, none ever appeared. The list was rather like an amulet, a way of calling on the magical power of the number one hundred to insure him long life.

The final bit of magic on the signature page of the *One Hundred Views* is the curious seal that Hokusai here uses for the first time, the form of Mt. Fuji over what Japanese writers seem to have interpreted as stylized mist,[24] but what must surely be the trigram for "Lake" from the *I Ching*. If Fuji is taken as the sign for "Mountain," then the entire seal becomes the hexagram known as "Decrease" (*son*). It is impossible to know exactly what this might have meant to Hokusai, but a plausible interpretation would see the "decrease" as representing Hokusai's own declining years, which would be compensated for by the immortality that he sought in the power of Mt. Fuji above. The sense of the "Lake" as water, giving off evaporation to benefit the mountains, is reflected in the frequency with which Hokusai depicts water in the foreground of his views of Fuji.

One final question is why the *One Hundred Views of Mt. Fuji* in fact contains a total of 102 separate views, divided 31–30–41 among the three volumes. Why the extra two, and why the imbalance among the separate volumes? Suzuki suggests that the initial plan called for four volumes, but the distribution between the first two volumes makes this unlikely. Possibly Hokusai was simply careless, putting too many two-page spreads in the first two volumes and was thus forced to cram the remaining ones into the third, resulting in more single-page designs in that volume. Such practical concerns may explain the large number of separate views in Volume III, but not the extra two. Perhaps, as one scholar has suggested, Hokusai simply had an intuitive dislike of completion.[25] In this particular instance, however, I think that the two beyond one hundred were related to his underlying preoccupation with long life: they were like the "one to grow on" candle that we stick in a birthday cake, a wish that he actually live on past his cherished goal of one hundred.

The Book

In viewing the *One Hundred Views of Mt. Fuji*, it helps to understand its character as a physical artifact, since a reproduction of the sort offered here cannot completely replicate the original. It is a book in three separate volumes: each roughly six inches wide, nine inches high, and one-quarter inch thick. In the traditional Japanese manner, it is composed of woodblock-printed pages that are folded in half and bound along the outer edges with silk string; each volume consists of twenty-seven such folios except for Volume III, which lacks a final colophon page. The center column along which each sheet is folded is known as the "pillar" (*hashira*) and consists of a mini-Fuji pattern followed by the title of the book and volume number, and, near the bottom, a dividing line and folio number. This information is neatly split into halves when folded, leaving a generally legible trace on either side and an artful reminder of the physical continuity of each sheet.

Each volume was bound between covers of heavy paper. In the first edition of Volumes I and II these are a salmon pink color on which is imprinted in a faintly darker shade a depiction of the Eight Views of Omi—a familiar landscape theme here executed (perhaps not by Hokusai himself) in a stylized way. A vertical label, printed in indigo, appears to the upper left of the front cover, with the title of the book—*Fugaku hyakkei*—enclosed in the stylized design of a falcon feather (Fig. 1). The volume number is specified for the second volume but not the first; no known example of the third volume appeared in this format. Books in this period were generally sold in a wrapper that encircled the book horizontally; this has survived for Volume I alone and is reproduced in Fig. 2. It features a handsome color-printed design of a falcon on a perch, whose braided leash is extended to provide a frame for the title, date, and artist's signature. The imagery of the falcon that appears both on the wrapper and the cover labels is surely related to the theme of the "Dream," which Hokusai depicts in No. 42, and carries through to the inside front cover design of eggplants in Volume I.

In its first edition, of which Volumes I and II in the Spencer Collection are good examples, the *One Hundred Views of Mt. Fuji* represents one of the triumphs of Japanese printing in woodblock. To begin with, the carving is astonishing, capturing the rhythms and nervous energy of Hokusai's brush without losing attention to minuteness of detail. Study the lines on the robes in No. 1, or the fingers of the seated figures in No. 2, or the hair on the pilgrims in No. 6, or the array of dots to the right in No. 9—and so on through all the remaining views—trying to feel the movements by which human fingers and a small knife could cut away the wood that would leave such animated dots and lines.

The carvers of the *One Hundred Views* are known by name. They worked under a master named Egawa Tomekichi, whose name alone appears on the colophon at the end of Volumes I and II. But to the bottom left of each "pillar"—that is, in the lower right margin of each right-hand page—appears the name of the individual carver of that folio. Seven different names appear for the fifty-one signed sheets in these two volumes; most numerous is "Esen," nickname for Egawa Sentarō. Volume III is different: it has no carver names on individual sheets, simply the notation "Carved by Egawa Sentarō" in the lower left margin of the last view (No. 102); it seems possible that this volume was in fact carved by a team but that Sentarō rather than his master Tomekichi was in charge when the volume was finally printed and removed all names but his own. At any rate, Hokusai, whose own early training as a carver made him picky about such matters, was pleased with the work done by the Egawa team, as he noted in a letter to one of his publishers in early 1835.[26]

The other technical accomplishment of the *One Hundred Views of Mt. Fuji* is the printing (although exception must be made for Volume III). After the main "key block" was printed in black sumi ink, one or two additional blocks were carved for the tones of gray (simply diluted sumi), and it is these subtle variations of gray shading against sharp black lines that account for the special aesthetic of the first edition. In two instances (Nos. 36 and 52), an extra black block was used to special effect. But it is the use of the gray that is so distinctive and so effective, whether in the overlay of lighter and darker shades or in the use of gradation (*bokashi*) by the wiping of the color on the block.

It is in the context of the printing of gray that it would be best to touch on the problem of Volume III, which is anomalous in the lack of a colophon that might provide a date. Nor do any of the surviving editions have covers like those on the first impressions of the two previous volumes; that in the Spencer Collection, for example, is an undecorated yellow.[27] We know from the preface and the advertisements on the inside covers that it was published by Tōhekidō (the famous Eirakuya Tōshirō) of Nagoya, rather than by Seirindō in Edo, publisher of the first edition of Volumes I and II.

The primary internal clue to the dating of Volume III is in the preface, where the author Shippōsanka Rōjin (whose identity is unknown) mentions that he has heard that Hokusai has reached the age of ninety—which would mean 1849, the year in which Hokusai died, on the eighteenth day of the Fourth Month. Any date for Volume III later than 1835, however, would seem to be contradicted by Hokusai's previously mentioned letter to a publisher in the second month of that year, in which he indicated that the *One Hundred Views of Mt. Fuji* had already been carved "from Volume I through Volume III." Some have accepted this as proof of publication shortly after Volume II in 1835, claiming that the mention of age ninety is an error. But if so, it is a very big error, given Hokusai's careful concern for his age at any given time; it is hard to see how even second-hand information could have confused seventy-six and ninety.

I prefer Suzuki Jūzō's ingenious explanation for the mystery of Volume III. His theory was inspired by the observation that the design of the gray patterns in this volume is generally awkward and utterly different from those in the first two; note, for example, the ragged clouds in Nos. 63 and 70, or the blotchy snow on Mt. Fuji in Nos. 77 and 82. What happened, Suzuki suggests, is that the blocks for all three volumes were indeed carved as of early 1835, as Hokusai said in his letter—but only the key blocks. The first two volumes came out as planned, but the publisher Seirindō ran into some trouble in the meantime, most plausibly related to the famine that reached a peak in Edo in 1837. So the blocks for Volume III sat unused, and with no gray blocks yet cut. Years passed and the key blocks passed into the hands of Tōhekidō in Nagoya, the co-publisher of Hokusai's famous *Manga* and also one of the distributors of the first two volumes of the *One Hundred Views*. Perhaps Hokusai had left only rough sketches for the gray blocks and was too old (or simply unavailable) to produce the finished designs. Whatever the reason, the publisher found someone else to do the job—someone of clearly inferior talent.[29]

But can we really conclude that Volume III actually appeared in 1849, the year of Hokusai's death? Matthi Forrer offers two pieces of evidence that in fact suggest a somewhat earlier date. Most important is the list of Tōhekidō publications on the inside front cover of the earliest impressions, which Forrer dates to 1840–47 (type "D"). He was also able to identify "Shippō Sanka Rōjin," the author of the preface to Volume III, as the writer of other Tōhekidō prefaces in the 1840s; the style of signature most closely corresponding to that of Volume III appears in a preface dated 1847.[28] The case remains tentative, but it seems plausible that the author of the preface really meant that Hokusai "is about to pass ninety years," rather than "has already passed ninety years." Hence Volume III probably appeared in 1847 or shortly before.

The Views

No one can fail to be impressed by the ingenious variety of guises in which Hokusai manages to represent the sacred peak. This is more than a game for the artist, despite a certain spirit of playful wit. Rather, it is at heart an extended demonstration that Mt. Fuji by way of its form maintains the power to remain unchanged in spite of the constant change that surrounds it. It is like the focus of Hokusai's Myōken faith and the source of his very name: the North Star, which remains fixed and immovable as the heavens rotate about it. By thus standing apart from the world of phenomenal change, Fuji transcends all change: it becomes, in short, Immortal.

One key element to this logic is Hokusai's essentially platonic belief in the inner truth of geometrical form, a belief that cannot escape anyone who studies his later designs. He in fact made an explicit demonstration of this belief in the earliest of his several drawing manuals, the *Quick Primer on Sketching* (*Ryakuga hayaoshie*) of 1812.[30] The first volume of this two-volume work introduces a method of drawing by using compass and square to make circles and lines that establish the underlying form of a composition. It is likely, as Fumiko Tōgasaki has shown, that Hokusai was influenced, directly or indirectly, by some Western example, but the development of the concept is all Hokusai's own.[31] The preface by one "Bainen" makes the central proposition that "although there are various formulas for painting . . . , in the end they all originate in circles and squares." This may reflect an assertion by Mencius that "without the use of a compass or square one would not be able to make squares or circles,"[32] but Hokusai's interest was clearly less in the use of mechanical instruments (which he probably himself eschewed) than in the underlying truth of regular geometrical form. This belief is demonstrated again and again in the *One Hundred Views of Mt. Fuji*.

The obsession with pure form is reflected in a crucial, symbolic way in the frequent echoing of the form of Mt. Fuji in the human body, as seen most overtly in Nos. 60 and

70. The life-giving power of Fuji is thus expressed by the literal incorporation of its form into the human figure. Royall Tyler uses the word "oromorphize" (as opposed to "anthropomorphize," from the prefix oro–, "mountain") for this transformation, in effect, of man into the mountain.[33] Looking closely, we can see the form of Fuji being constantly reproduced in the human figure: in the arch of spine, in the closure of limbs, and on down to gestures of the hand (as in No. 2).

All that has been said so far applies as much to the *Thirty-Six Views of Mt. Fuji* as to the *One Hundred Views*. What sets the latter work apart is an expansion of Hokusai's methods of presenting Fuji *beyond* the standard landscape form. One such extension is into the realm of history, as seen in the opening views of Volume I, where the creation of the mountain, its ascent by En no Gyōja, and the Hōei eruption are all depicted. Thus we are given to understand that Mt. Fuji does indeed have a particular past, just as it is always seen from a particular place. But in the end, of course, it is beyond all time and place.

The treatment of specific place is also revealingly different from the *Thirty-Six Views*, in which particular place names were provided for all but three prints: revealingly, these include two of the most celebrated—the "Red Fuji" and "Thunderstorm Below the Mountain" (reinterpreted in Nos. 4 and 52)—and the one that shows not the mountain from afar, but as it was experienced by climbing pilgrims (redone as No. 46). In the *One Hundred Views*, there are, to be sure, a considerable number of titles with proper place names—a total of twenty-six, to be exact, of which twelve are in Edo and the rest elsewhere. Yet, there are recurring difficulties in finding any connection between the place of the title and the view to which it is attached. Sometimes, the place cannot be located (Nos. 49, 101); in others, the location is in doubt (Nos. 65, 74); in still others, obscure (Nos. 50, 79), or vague (No. 53), or difficult to recognize (Nos. 14, 41, 83, 90, 98), or largely imaginary (Nos. 62, 73, 92). Even when the place and scene are thoroughly familiar, as in the cherries at Mukōjima in No. 75, one senses a certain conscious distancing, an other-worldly ethos.

This links in turn with what I sense to be a visionary, even mystical quality in a number of views; I perceive this most strongly in Nos. 35 and 71, but it also appears elsewhere, and strengthens the argument that Hokusai was consciously rejecting the world of known places in favor of those generated by his imagination. In this way, he was universalizing his views of Fuji without sacrificing the sense of immediacy that the attentive detail of his views inspires.

If Hokusai relied largely on his imagination for his views, it of course does not necessarily follow that he was not inspired by places he actually visited on his travels in the area around Fuji: it simply means that he reconstituted these impressions in a wholly personal way. This contradicts the common assertion that Hokusai must have traveled widely in order to make preliminary sketches for *One Hundred Views of Mt. Fuji*.[34] The first to make this claim was his own publisher, who issued a single-sheet advertisement for the book in 1833—the year before the publication of Volume I—claiming that Hokusai had in the course of his travels accumulated a whole basketful of sketches of spectacular landscapes.[35] Similar sentiments are expressed in Ryūtei Tanehiko's preface to Volume I.

All of this, however, is no more than the standard rhetoric that was used in this period to tout *any* landscape prints, and tells us nothing whatsoever about the way in which Hokusai gathered his material. He certainly traveled around Fuji and perhaps made sketches of what he saw. But I frankly doubt it: the image of the avid sketch-artist that he shows in No. 47 is, as Tsuji Nobuo astutely suggests, a view of the ideal elite artist and not of Hokusai himself, who more likely sketched the *One Hundred Views of Mt. Fuji* in a tiny back-street tenement in downtown Edo. Some of his preliminary drawings for this work in fact survive, and none of them have the look of on-site sketches.[36]

This is not to say that Hokusai was unconcerned with the ways in which we actually see the world around us. On the contrary, one finds in the *One Hundred Views of Mt. Fuji* a number of intriguing prints that dwell on paradoxes of the visual world (such as reflections, in Nos. 20, 37, and 39, or the pinhole effect, in No. 99) and of the way it is transformed into pictures (Nos. 44, 47, 60). Hokusai was in a sense raising the most fundamental questions of what makes a picture, and thus by implication posing the philosophical question of the relationship between the pure form of Fuji and its physical reality.

For Hokusai, however, this sort of exercise was doubtless as much intellectual play as a serious inquiry into the philosophy of pictures. As suggested earlier, it seems more likely that the wit in such views involved a translation of poetic techniques, notably those of punning and allusion, into pictorial ones. Hokusai's only pastime other than painting seems to have been the composition of senryū, of which quite a number survive, and one of which seems perfectly suited to one of the *One Hundred Views* (see commentary on No. 70).

After One Hundred

Ironically, the highly celebratory *One Hundred Views of Mt. Fuji* began to appear at a time when things were getting bad for Hokusai and for Japan in general. By late 1834, the year in which Volume I appeared, Hokusai had left Edo for the Miura Peninsula, thirty miles south, in what seems to have been a self-imposed exile, for reasons that are unknown. Meanwhile, the famine, which had already been mounting when the first two volumes appeared in 1834–35, reached a peak of severity in 1837, resulting in widespread death and in the disruption of all print production in Edo (including, presumably, the third volume of the *One Hundred Views*). Hokusai in time returned to Edo, but in 1839 his studio was burned, and all of the designs he used for reference were destroyed.

And yet Hokusai remained undaunted, still productive, although now mostly in paintings rather than prints. He inevitably signed his paintings with his age, as he continued the countdown to the cherished age of one hundred, and made frequent pronouncements about his intention to achieve that goal. He began using a new seal in his late years that read simply "Hundred." Already famous for the number of times he changed his residence, he announced that he was aiming at one hundred moves (he made it to ninety-three). In 1842, at the age of eighty-three, he took up the practice of drawing a picture of a lion (or lion-dancer) every morning as a way of exorcising evil spirits and prolonging life. In an explanatory note attached to a group of these paintings when he gave them to an acquaintance in 1847, he took care to append the recipe for his own life-prolonging medicine, which may be worth passing on here:[37]

> Remove the skin from longan nuts [*ryūgan*, a close relative of the litchi, available from dealers in Chinese medicine] and weigh out two ounces; then combine with one ounce of refined white sugar and mix into two quarts of the highest grade of potato liquor [*shōchū*; vodka diluted to sixty proof could substitute], put in a jar, seal well, and put aside for sixty days. Then take two small sake-cups of the medicine every morning and every evening. This is a medicine for long life, thanks to which I have been able to live 88 years without illness.

In the end, Hokusai's countdown to one hundred fell just ten years short of the mark. On his deathbed in the Fourth Month of 1849, Iijima Kyoshin reported, "he gave a great sigh and said, 'If only I could have just another ten years.' Some time passed, and he spoke again 'just another five years—then I could become a real artist.'"[38] Whether true or not, the anecdote is perfectly in character.

As it turned out, Hokusai did of course achieve the immortality he sought, in the continuing life of his art. In the instance of the *One Hundred Views of Mt. Fuji*, the greatest appreciation seems to have come only after his death. It was only in Hiroshige's *One Hundred Famous Views of Edo* (1856–58), for example, that one can find any persuasive evidence of designs by Japanese artists that were inspired by Hokusai's.[39]

But as time passed, the popularity of the *One Hundred Views* grew steadily, as evidenced by the constant reprinting of the work. The history of these reprints is complex but the basic outline may be reconstructed from the studies of Suzuki Jūzō and Matthi Forrer.[40] The original "falcon tail" edition of Volumes I–II went through at least one more impression in Edo (see commentary on colophon of Volume II), presumably before the famine of 1837. Both volumes were then re-issued with different covers and no colophons by Tōhekidō in Nagoya at the time of the first publication of Volume III in the late 1840s. At least one more impression of all three volumes together followed.

Then, sometime in the 1850s, a different edition was introduced by Tōhekidō, in which completely new color blocks were designed, one in gray and one in a salmon pink.[41] Not only was a true color added, but also the patterns of the blocks were wholly different. The result may be seen as a betrayal of Hokusai's original intentions, but at least the key blocks were still in fairly good condition, and some of the resulting designs and color combinations have a special appeal of their own.

In the 1860s or early 1870s, however, the Nagoya publisher decided to reissue the work with the original gray blocks which had been preserved. Forrer indicates that the earliest versions of these had the color blocks printed in "bluish gray." Next came impressions dated December, 1875 and January, 1876 with the same blocks in normal gray sumi. The blocks passed at some unknown later date into the hands of the Tokyo publisher Yoshikawa Hanshichi and were printed still again. The original blocks, badly worn, survived into the twentieth century and were reprinted in Tokyo for one last time in 1943 by Unsōdō.[42] The long-lived blocks may in fact still survive today, although no one

I asked would say for sure. After the war, two facsimile versions were published: one in woodblock by Unsōdō in 1964–65,[43] based on the edition with additional pink colors, and one in photographic reproduction by Iwasaki Bijutsusha in 1972, from a fine first edition, with Suzuki Jūzō's authoritative commentaries.

The *One Hundred Views of Mt. Fuji* was introduced to the West at an early point. Two of the views (Nos. 35 and 53) were reproduced in lithograph in a report of 1861 by a French ambassador to Japan, Baron Charles de Chassiron. Two decades later, Frederick Dickins wrote a detailed commentary on *One Hundred Views*, including translations of the prefaces and comments on each view. It is easy today to smile at Dickins's numerous errors of translation and interpretation, but well to note that this volume was probably the first scholarly study of Hokusai ever to be published—in any format or in any language. (The serious Japanese study of the artist would begin only with Iijima Kyoshin's landmark biography of 1893.) Less admirable was its reprinting in 1958 by a New York publisher that included a photographic reproduction of a good early edition—most of whose pages are printed in mirror image so that the book could be read from left to right! The result is upsetting and provides persuasive evidence that lateral orientation is crucial to Japanese design.

Over a century and a half has now passed since Hokusai's masterpiece first appeared, and it is to be hoped that this new reproduction of a fine edition of the *One Hundred Views of Mt. Fuji* from an American collection will encourage a new and deeper understanding of Hokusai and his talismanic celebration of the great mountain from which he sought—and found—immortality.

NOTES

[1] Hokusai used many more than the basic six names of Shunrō, Sōri, Hokusai, Taito, Iitsu, and Manji; but I here accept the argument of Yasuda Gōzō that he formally announced changes of name only five times. See Yasuda (1971) and his "Hokusai kaimei kō," in Suzuki, et al. (1972): 19–28.

[2] Ishigami (1985): 1145.

[3] For the history of the religious cult of Fuji, see Inobe (1983).

[4] Ogawa (1985): 66.

[5] Kobayashi (1976): 62–63.

[6] See Keene translation (1955): 354–55.

[7] Nagata, ed. (1986), 5: 150–153. The title of this work is often read *Imayō kushi kiseru hiinagata*; I have followed Nagata, however, in using the reading provided by the kana glosses in the postscript to vol. 3 (199).

[8] Ibid., 260.

[9] Narazaki (1944): 35.

[10] Suzuki (1963): 62–64. These prints are undated, but a publisher's advertisement of 1831 suggests that the series had recently begun; the total of 46 prints was probably completed by 1833. My own sense of the advertisement is that the series had just begun, probably no earlier than 1830.

[11] Translation from de Bary, et al. (1960): 24.

[12] Narazaki (1944): 403–406. Nagata (1971): 24 suggests that the theory began with Oda Kazuma (1926), but I have been unable to locate any trace of it in that work.

[13] Nagata (1971) and Suzuki (1986): 183–84. Suzuki had offered an indirect criticism of the theory in *Ningen Hokusai:* (1963): 80–83.

[14] Kojima (1931): 84.

[15] Shimizu Hanaomi [1776–1824], ed., "Minasedono Fuji hyakushu," ms., n.d.; listed in *Kokusho sōmokuroku.* Ujinari's date of death is given by Takeshima (1920): 13.

[16] See: Hassenbō ed., *Hyaku Fuji* [1806]; Ichiryōken Sonomaru, ed., *Kyōka hyaku Fuji Saburō* [1817];Torigoe Tsunenari, *Fuji hyakushi* [1819]; and Sumida Teichō, ed., *Fuji hyakushu waka* [1831]. All appear in *Kokusho sōmokuroku,* which however gives a publication date of 1830 for *Kyōka hyaku Fuji saburō;* the date of 1817, which is given in Takayanagi (1929): 70, most likely represents an earlier impression.

[17] The most extended argument for Minsetsu's influence on Hokusai's views of Fuji is Iso (1961).

[18] Takeuchi (1983): 179–80.

[19] Yasuda (1971): 172.

[20] Yoshida (1974), 3: 98.

[21] This work is reported in *Kokusho sōmokuroku* to be in the National Diet Library in Tokyo, but I have been unable to examine it.

[22] Freed and Freed (1980).

[23] Narazaki, et al. (1982): 131 implies that there may be a special meaning of the swastika in the Nichiren sect of Buddhism to which Hokusai belonged, but he does not specify.

[24] Yasuda (1971): 177.

[25] Tsuji (1982): 137.

[26] The letter appears in Iijima (1893), 1: fols. 54–56.

[27] What appears to be the earliest impression of Volume III is reported by Forrer [(1985): 173] to have an "orange" cover and by Suzuki [1986: 195] to have a "red-orange [*tan*]" cover; it is unclear if they are identical. The Spencer copy is clearly later, judging both from the wear on the key blocks and from the later advertisements (Forrer's pattern E3/40, which he dates to the period 1850–59). It

would seem to correspond to the version that Forrer identifies as a "variant state" of the earliest impression of the "Second Edition," probably just prior to the version with the new gray and pink blocks.

[28] Forrer (1985): 102, 149. The other work is *Shinji andō*, with a preface by "Shippō Sanka Sōan Kogasa [Shōryū?]."

[29] Suzuki (1986): 205 proposes that the job may have been done by a follower of Hokusai in the Nagoya area.

[30] This work is reproduced in Nagata, ed. (1986), vol. 5.

[31] Tōgasaki (1976) part 2: 19–26.

[32] Nagata, in particular, relies on this theme in his articles of 1971 and 1972.

[33] Ware translation, chap. 4A, 1. This suggestion comes from Tsuji (1982): 118.

[34] Tyler (1981): 144.

[35] This advertisement is known only from a reproduction in Narazaki (1944): 416.

[36] The preliminary sketches for Nos. 36, 52, and 57 are reproduced in Hillier (1980): 222–25.

[37] Narazaki (1944): 451.

[38] Iijima (1893), 1: fol. 67.

[39] See Smith (1986): pls. 73 and 75 for works that were inspired, respectively, by Nos. 12 and 38.

[40] Suzuki (1986): 187-197 and Forrer (1985): 170–177.

[41] This edition may be dated both from the appearance of advertisement type "E3" which Forrer dates 1850–59, and from the fact that two reproductions from it appear in Chassiron (1861).

[42] Suzuki [1986: 197] notes that this edition, which I have not seen, was accompanied by a commentary by Kojima Usui that was basically the same as that in his 1931 book, pp. 84–95. Suzuki appears to be in error, however, in giving the date of this edition as 1948; see Harigaya, et al. (1972): 111.

[43] Forrer, p. 177, misreads Suzuki in claiming that this edition "was still from the original line blocks"; a comparison with earlier editions makes it clear that all the blocks were recut, and that it should be considered a reproduction, not a new edition. It included a separate pamphlet with the Kawakita commentary listed in the Bibliography.

One Hundred Views
of Mt. Fuji

NOTE

In this edition of the *One Hundred Views of Mt. Fuji*, the plates
have been placed according to the oriental tradition of bookmaking,
that is, from "back to front" to the western reader. The reader
should turn to page 191 in order to view the illustrations in the
sequence that Hokusai intended and for which they were designed.

煎茶早指南　尾礫舍 主人著　月樵老人畫　全一冊

此書ハ煎茶の極意を殘しなく記すなり煎茶を初めてきく人も道具揃ハざる
更等を好ふたふわらば道具ハ有合のものふて心安く調へ客来るとても恥
うからざる樣小工風を盡し就中煎茶の水加減ハ朝夕小開める小大小益
より番茶の煮るも此煎法を以て増減をかる時ハ百茶も裏じて妙撰一味
夢の瓜の高味を尽べ巻中小委しく見えそゝ

俳諧五七集　枇杷園士朗翁著　全五冊

士朗先生俳諧の書数篇の中三十五部をふて五七集と号け先生一世の
俳諧風雅を尽されＬ山書たり芭蕉翁いろひの一大家ふて風調意味
深く此道小遊ぶ輩の亀鑑とすべしＬ

書肆

尾州名古屋本町通七丁目　永樂屋東四郎
江戸日本橋通本銀町二丁目　同　出店

大尾一筆
此不二

蛇退沼の不二

III / 101

海濱の不二

千束の不二

32

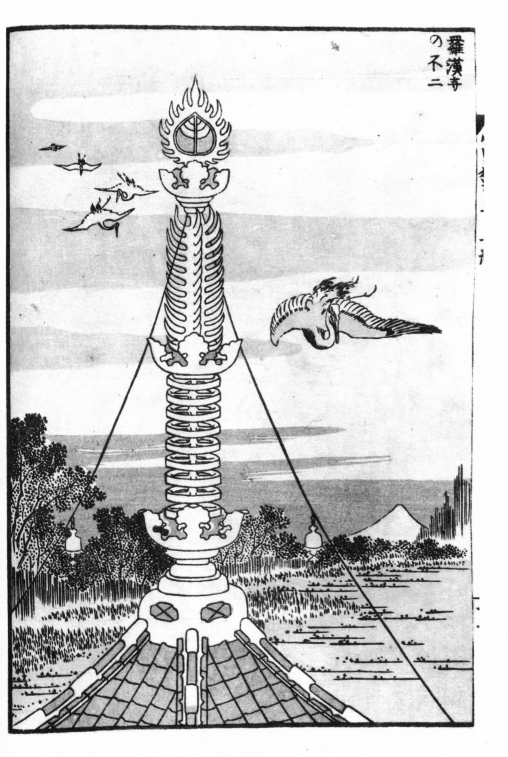

郭
え
の
不
二

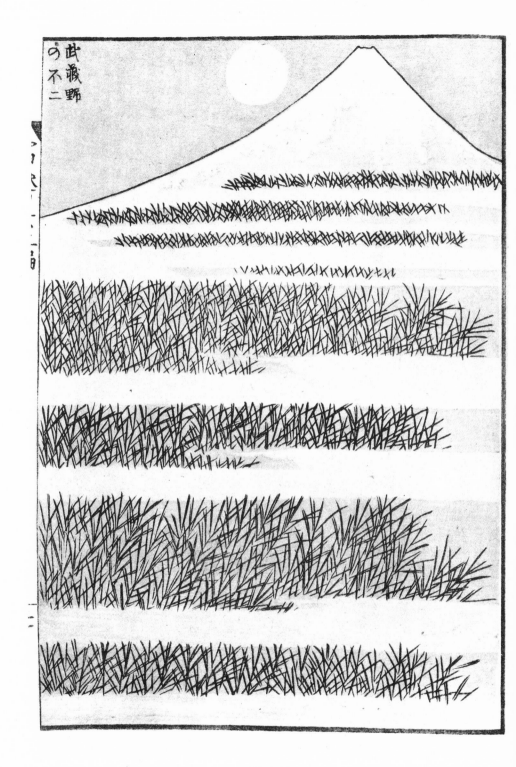

武蔵野の不二

や社ぬるにる里ちよ花さけたりふる

大井川桶越の不二

福
録
寿

III / 89

41

狼煙の不二

橋下の不二

村堺の不二

鳥越の不二

稲毛領
其の不二

甲斐の不二
濃男

III / 76

良哈

兀

水道橋の不二

暁の不二

III / 68

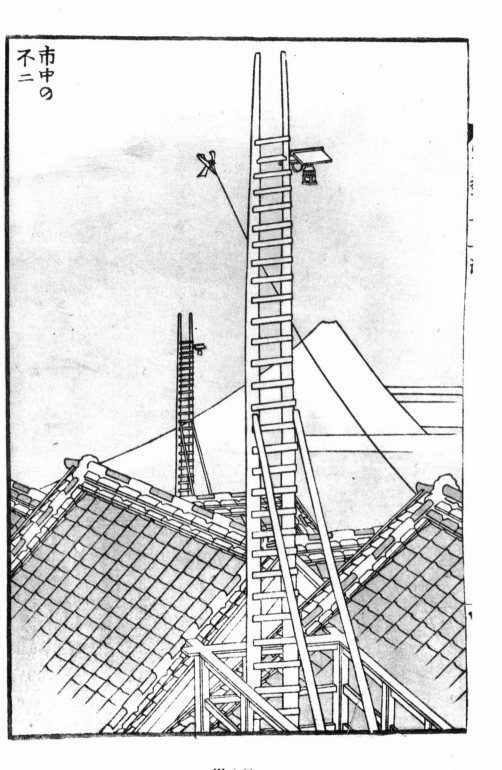

市中の不二

砂村の不二
貴家別莊

深雪の不二

野列遠景の不二

男體山
行者戻の松

赤澤の不二

朕野五郎國久

河津三郎祐安

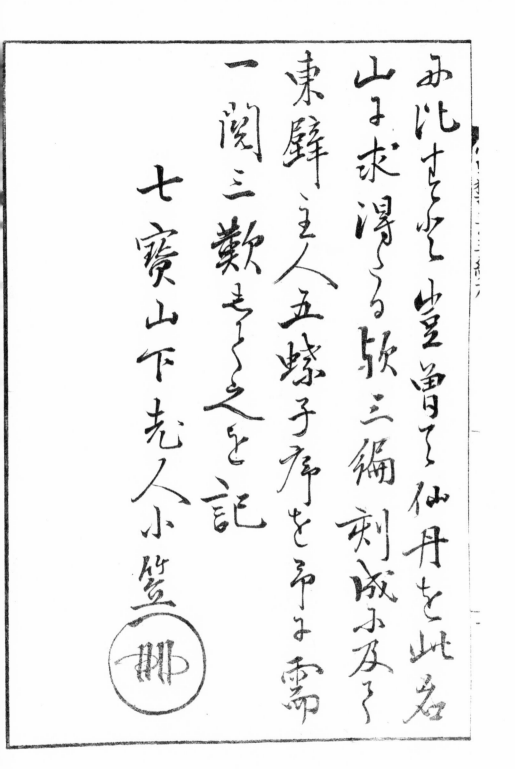

此さ空曾て仙丹を此名
山を求得る歌三編剞劂成小及て
東辟主人五蝶子序を市る需
一閲三歎もてくを記
七寶山下老人小笠

君錫子の百富士を畫乃正たらふ
えたる北齋翁の富嶽正景八
畫乃齋うる者より翁雄健く
筆をにて一富峰をよく楷墨の
間を鼓舞す八面向背寫し得く
きはめて紗絶まり聞翁の齢
今九十を踰て視聴な弐少年

III / Preface

尾張東壁堂藏板画譜畫手本目録

北齋漫画　狂画苑　北齋画譜

北溪漫画　文鳳麁画　同　中編

北雲漫画　蕙齋麁画　同　下編

珖琳漫画　神事行燈　富嶽百景

金氏画譜　北齋女今川　同　二編

一筆画譜　初學繪手本　同　三編

英勇画譜　福善齋画譜　繪本庭訓

浮世画譜　武勇魁圖繪　同　中編

英泉画譜　浮世画手本　同　下編

III / Inside Front Cover

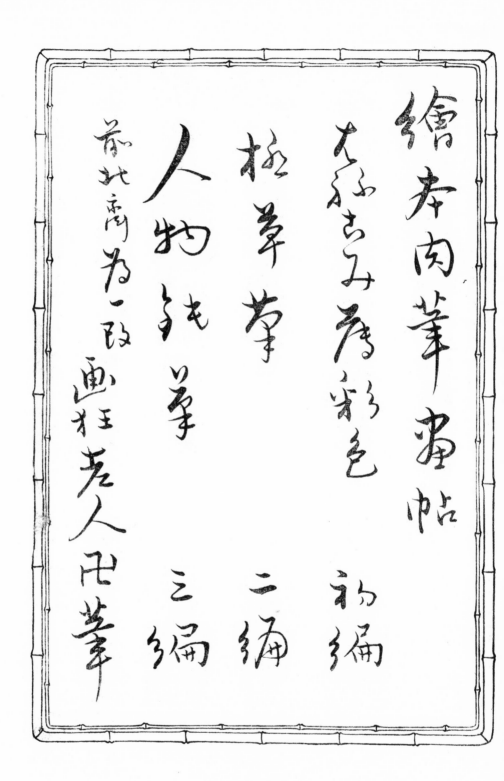

繪本肉筆畫帖

大和絵志み廣彩色　　初編

極草筆　　　　　二編

人物鈍筆　　　三編

希此齊為一政画狂老人卍筆

漁家百景　近刻

月下百景　同

農家百景　同

圓方長短一百自在圖會　近刻

百馬百牛　同

百禽百獸　同

天保六乙未年春三月發行

書林

尾州名古屋　永樂屋東四郎

江戸麴町四丁目　角丸屋甚助

仝馬喰町二丁目　西村與八

仝　西村祐藏

七十六齢　前北齋為一改　画狂老人卍筆

己六才より物の形状を写の癖ありて半百の比より數々画圖を顯すといへども七十年前畫く所々実に取にたるものなし七十三才より稍禽獸虫魚の骨格草木の出生を悟し得たり故に八十才にしては益々進み九十才にして猶其奥意を極め一百歳にして正に神妙ならん歟百有十歳にしては一點一格にして生るがごとくあらん願くは長壽の君子予が言の妄ならざるを見給ふべし

画狂老人卍述

剖劂　江川留吉　五榮堂

富嶽百景　二編初編　三編

名橋百景　近刻

異草百花撰　近刻

百家奇術　同

狂画草筆百眼　同

百壽百福　同

II / Colophon

82

武邊の不二

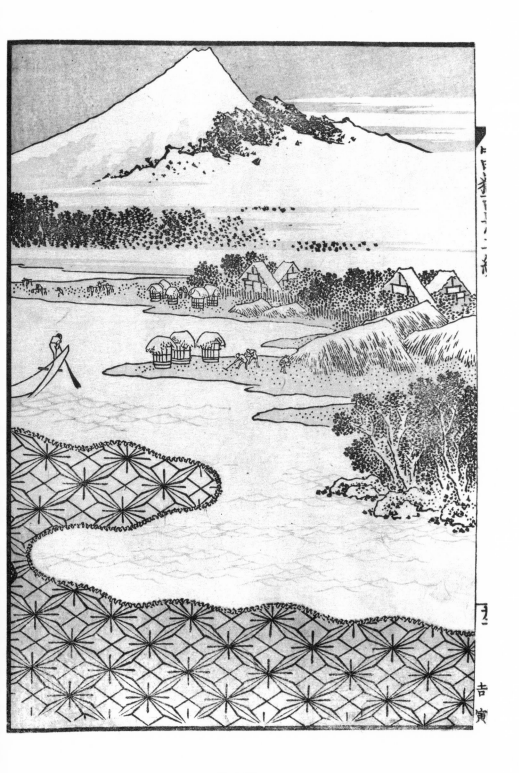

雪比且の不二

II / 55

筧の不二

遠江山中七
不二

夕立の不二

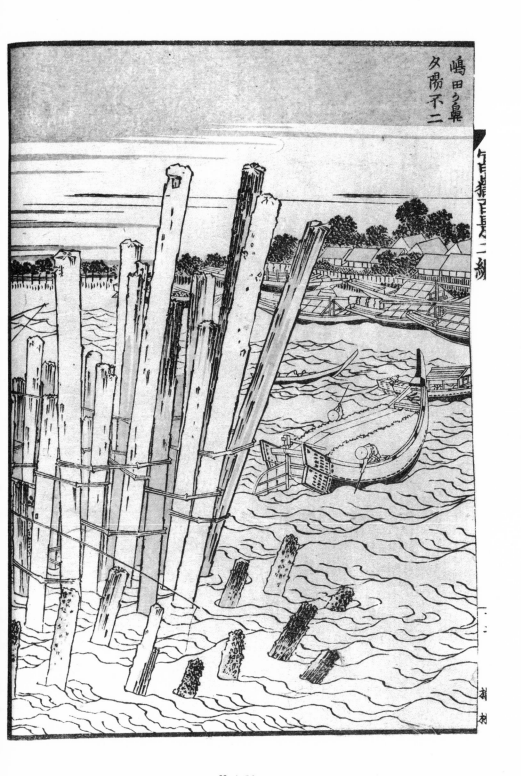

嶋田の鼻
夕陽不二

大石寺之山中の不二

106

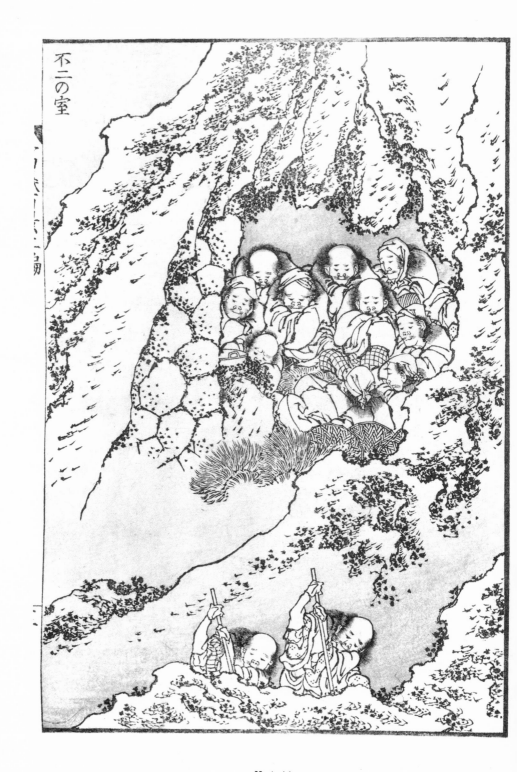

不二の室

松越の不二

夢の不二

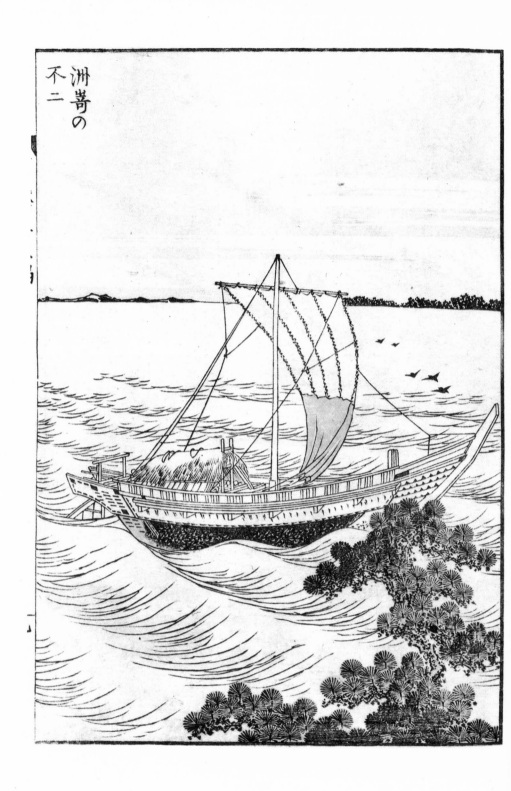

洲嵜の不二

盃中の不二

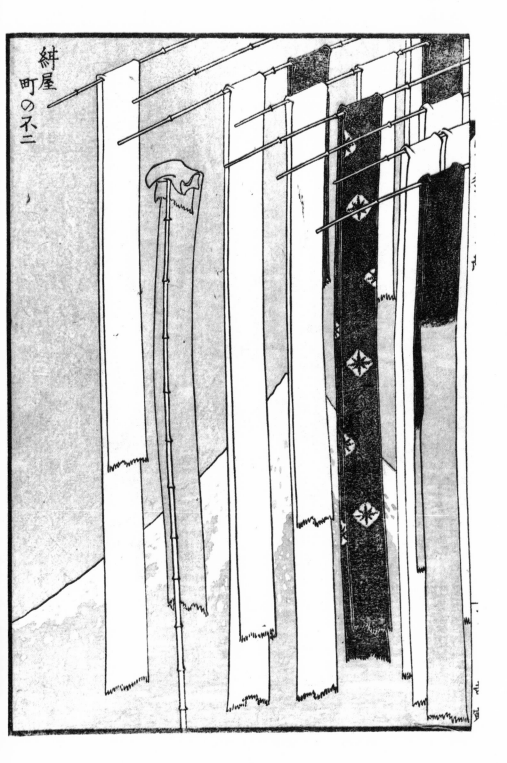

絣屋町の不二

登龍の不二

128

竹林の不二

信州八ケ嶽　其二

井戸浚の不二

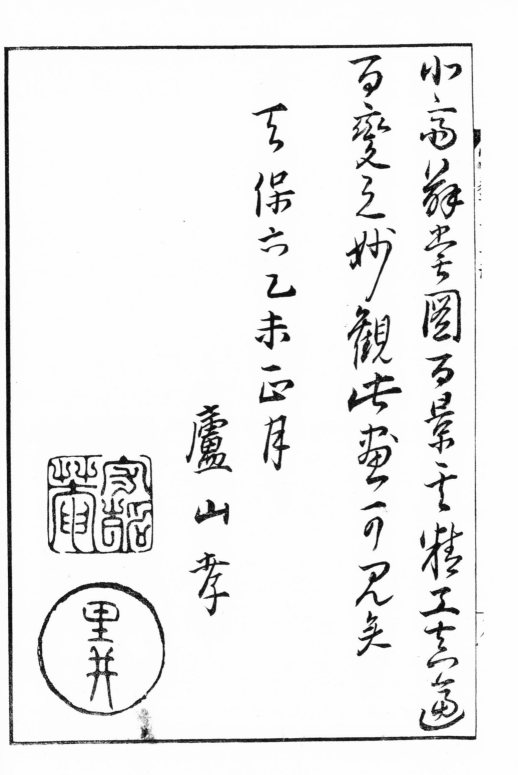

富士之为山也其形若冠玉若
磨銀焉而高聳不時不似八面玲
瓏如芙蓉之出水而高跨乎群嶽之
巔是千所以冠天...而盖夫...嶂
峽而皎潔夕陽谷与蒼翠相映蒼
變其色遠之笑而望金不春烟
秋風雲霧縹緲則其東西南北變又矣

富士散言録二編　序

II / Title Page (Inside Front Cover)

漁家百景　近刻

月下百景　同

農家百景　同

圓方長短一百自在圖會　近刻

百馬百牛　同

百禽百獸　同

天保五甲午年春三月發行

書林

尾州名古屋　永樂屋東四郎

江戸麹町四丁目　角丸屋甚助

仝馬喰町二丁目　西村與八

仝　西村祐藏

I / Colophon

七十五齢 前北齋為一改
画狂老人卍筆

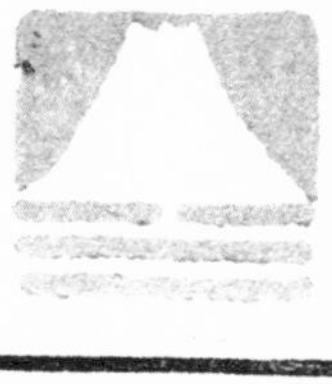

己六才より物の形状を写の癖ありて半百の比より数々画図を顕すといへども七十年前画く所は実に取に足ものなし七十三才にして稍禽獣虫魚の骨格草木の出生を悟し得たり故に八十才にしては益々進み九十才にして猶其奥意を極め一百歳にして正に神妙ならん歟百有十歳にしては一点一格にして生るがごとくならん願くは長寿の君子予が言の妄ならざるを見たまふべし

画狂老人卍述

剞劂 江川留吉 五常亭

冨嶽百景 初編既行 二編近刻 三編仝

名橋百景 近刻

異草百花撰 近刻

百家奇術 同

狂画草筆百眼 同

百壽百福 同

冨嶽百景初編

I / Colophon

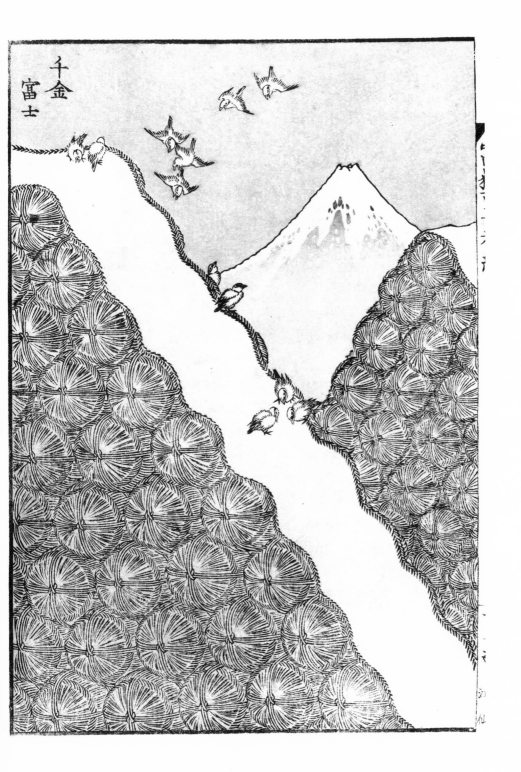

花間の不二

裏不二

米吉

鏡臺不二

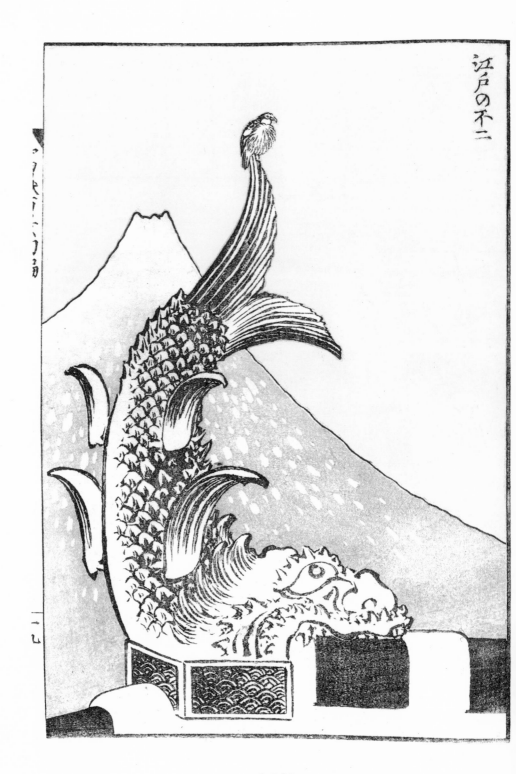

I / 24

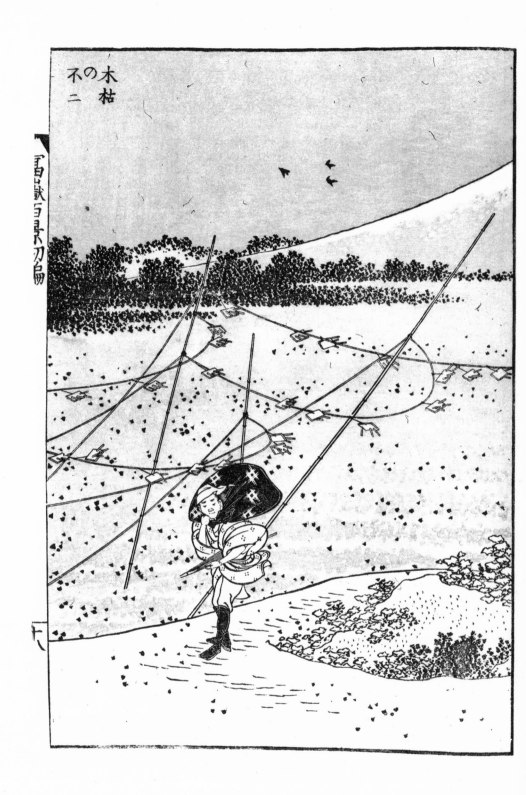

田面の不二

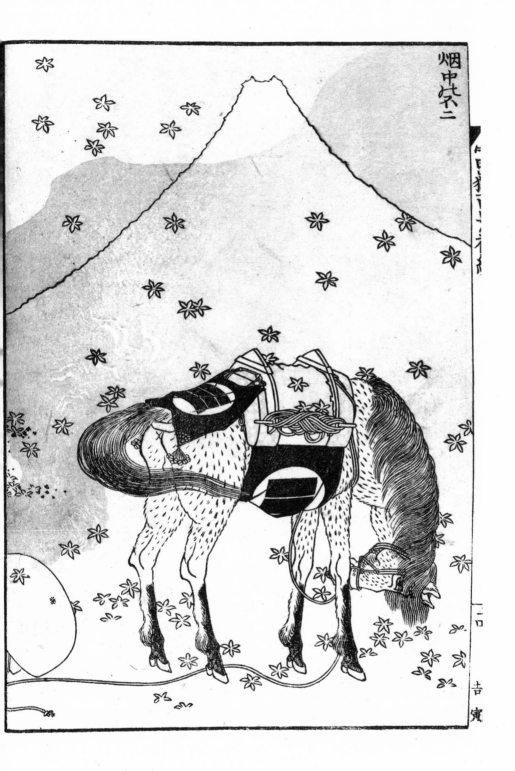

松山の
不二

吉
寅

洞中の不二

大森

尾州
不二見原

袖ヶ浦

山中の不二

霧中の不二

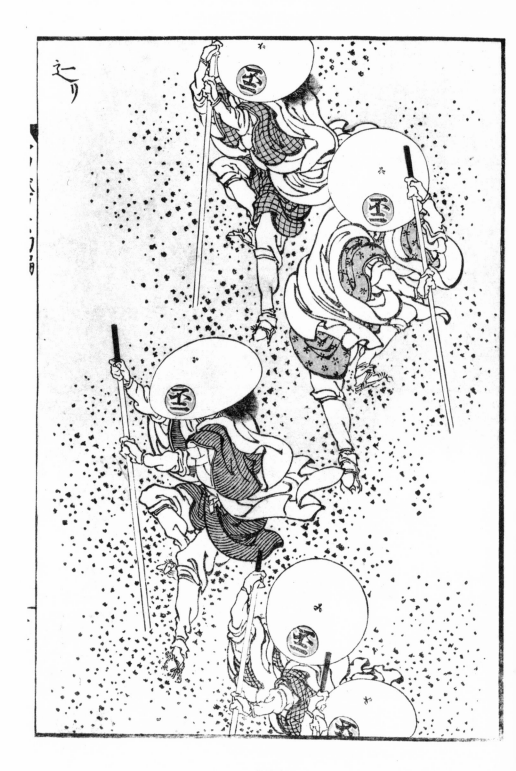

不二の明山

快晴の不二

182

I / 4

役ノ優婆塞
富嶽草創

木花開耶姫命

柳亭種彦書

天保甲午孟春

勢沖ゟ富士百首を室元述一字顕ホ
東流の不二雨らをく線雪みかく見えぬ
本料ゟ百嶽を圖をる八扇此齊物之此山や
獨立して六峰其頭半出一屏の畫も又物立
志を言名言事一子五るるよりさ如む
畫帖諸圖みゆ川蔵を里をる郡る堂
十五州の壮観るあむや不る十名を秘蔵わ
小戴するゟ先生屬名らろくな屬十なみ
壽海藝へ抬を入田に遣ひおむ此岳藝るて
年ゐゟ近々田み浦に見るへ三保ゟ時と

I / Title Page (Inside Front Cover)

🐚 Commentaries on the Plates 🐚

The following is the third set of complete commentaries on the *One Hundred Views of Mt. Fuji*, and I owe a debt to both of my predecessors. Frederick V. Dickins in 1880 was far more often wrong than right in everything that he wrote about the work; but he was a pioneer, and even his errors helped draw my attention to issues I might otherwise have neglected. My debt is far heavier to Suzuki Jūzō, whose commentaries of 1972 represent the only serious scholarship ever devoted to Hokusai's masterpiece. I have tried to indicate those instances in which I have particularly drawn on his interpretations.

The romanization of the Japanese titles often involves arbitrary choices between alternative readings; in general, I have preferred the Sino-Japanese (*on*) readings.

Volume I

🐚 *Title Page* (Inside Front Cover)

Whereas wrapper of Volume I features a falcon (fig. 1) and the title slip on the outside cover is in the form of a falcon feather (fig. 2), the title is here bordered by an eggplant (evident only by a close comparison with No. 42). Thus Hokusai completes the triangle of the three objects that bring good luck if seen in one's first dream of the year: Fuji, a falcon, and an eggplant. Hokusai later illustrates this theme in No. 42, but sets an auspicious tone to his volume by this witty incorporation of the proverb into the titling motifs.

Wrapper of Volume I, *One Hundred Views of Mt. Fuji* (1834). From Kojima Usui, *Edo makki no ukiyo-e* (Azusa shobō, 1931)

"Falcon feather" Title slip, Volume I, *One Hundred Views of Mt. Fuji* (1834).

The title of the book, *Fugaku hyakkei*, appears in the center. The seal to the upper right reads "Marvel of Painting" (*tansei no myō*); it must have had some personal connection with either Hokusai or his publisher. The formal store name of the latter, Seirindō, appears to the left, with an official "Seal of Publication" (*hatsuda no in*).

❦ Preface to Volume I

The collector's seal in the lower right margin indicates that this volume was once in the "Miyagawa Library" (Miyagawa bunko), which I have not been able to identify.

The translation of the preface is as follows: Keichū's *Hundred Verses on Fuji*[1] soars like a lofty peak, while the *One Hundred Haiku on Fuji by Tōchō*[2] remains hidden behind the many-colored clouds. Now it is the Former Hokusai who has pictured anew the hundred peaks. This one mountain stands apart, towering above the many lesser peaks; so also Old Man Hokusai's pictures stand apart, as high in fame as the fifteen thousand feet of Fuji. His albums are cherished throughout the country, beyond the Fifteen Provinces.[3]

Ten names for Fuji are recorded in the *Hizōshō*,[4] and Old Man Hokusai has frequently changed his own name, no less than ten times. Perhaps there is a connection here, for he has adored the peak of Fuji for many years. He must have thought that it was too trite to look up at Fuji from Tago Bay or across from Miho, as obvious as full blossoms under the cloudless moon. So he has walked with cane in hand as far as Fujimigahara and has parked his palanquin at Shiomizaka.[5] He has gazed up at the lofty peak through trailing willows and through trembling sheaves of rice. We see the open sea with waves beating against the rocks, winding roads buried in valleys white with mist, the ascent of precipitous hills and descent along perilous slopes. Since he has thus shown the true face of nature, his spirit resides in this volume.

Of all the many volumes of picture books, this one will surely stand above the rest, no less than do the hundred poems of [Keichū] Ajari.

> Respectfully,
> Ryūtei Tanehiko[6]
> [Seal: A die with "Hiko" on three sides]
> Abundant Green,[7] Tenpō Year of the Horse
> [1834]
> Calligraphy by Tōsai Moriyoshi[8]
> [Seals: Moriyoshi, Naokata]

Notes to Preface

[1] The title here (*Fukisan hyakushu*) is an abbreviation of *Ei Fujisan hyakushu waka* ("One Hundred Waka in Praise of Mt. Fuji"). It was published in printed editions in 1781, 1799, 1800, 1833, and 1836. Keichū (1640–1701) was a Buddhist priest and scholar whose formative studies into early Japanese literature laid the ground for the National Learning (Kokugaku) movement.

[2] This must refer to *Tōchō Fuji hyaku*, a collection of one hundred haiku on Fuji by Wada Tōchō (1658–1706). The work was published in 1692 and appears to have been little known, which may be the point Tanehiko is making here.

[3] By tradition, Mt. Fuji was visible from fifteen (sometimes thirteen) different provinces.

[4] Also known as *Kokin uchigiki* or *Waka hizōshō*, this is a fifteenth-century text on waka composition that concludes with the "Ten Names of Fuji" (Fuji jūmei), a list of ten poetic terms that could be used to describe Mt. Fuji (see *Zoku gunsho ruijū*, *kan* 456). Here it is simply a device used to make a parallel with Hokusai's habit of using many different art names.

[5] Hokusai does show a view from Fujimigahara (see No. 14), but not from Shiomizaka, or "Ocean View Hill," a stretch of the Tōkaidō highway just east of Shirasuka (now Kosai, Shizuoka Prefecture) known for the view and often mentioned in poetry. I suspect that Tanehiko was cribbing one of the prefaces to Kawamura Minsetsu's *Hyaku Fuji* of 1767, in which a similar passage, including the phrase "stopping his horse at Shiomizaka," appears.

[6] Ryūtei Tanehiko (1783–1842) was a well-known literary scholar and author of light fiction, a number of whose books had been illustrated by Hokusai, and who knew the artist well.

[7] "Abundant Green" (*ryokushū*) suggests early summer, but the publication date of the Third Month means that it must here indicate late spring.

[8] Matsumoto Tōsai (d. 1870) was a calligrapher of the late Tokugawa period who presumably had ties with Tanehiko or the publisher.

❦ 1. The Goddess Konohana Sakuya Hime
(Konohana Sakuya hime no mikoto)

This is the goddess of Fuji, hovering in the heavens like the peak itself, surrounded by fluffy clouds. In her right hand she holds a mirror, a Shinto symbol of purity and hence divinity, and in the left a branch of the sacred *sakaki* tree. In her hair is an ornament of a stylized butterfly. The gowns are drawn in a vibrant, nervous manner distinctive to Hokusai, and we sense the branch of *sakaki* to be growing directly from the being of the goddess. The very name Konohana Sakuya Hime in fact links this goddess to growth and fertility: "Princess of the Flowering of Tree Blossoms." She appears in chapter 41 of the *Kojiki*, the great eighth-century compilation of Japanese myth, as a goddess of unsurpassed beauty who gave birth to her child in a flaming palace, thereby proving the legitimacy of the child to her suspicious husband.

Many centuries passed, however, before this deity of early myth came to be associated specifically with Mt. Fuji, a process which occurred at the unrecorded level of folk belief in the late medieval period, from the fourteenth to sixteenth centuries. It was natural to choose a feminine deity, since early literary accounts had linked Fuji with a woman. The *Chronicle of Mt. Fuji* (Fujisan ki, c. 877), for example, told of the apparition of two white-robed women near the summit, and the "Tale of the Bamboo Cutter" (Taketori monogatari) of the same era concluded with the celestial heroine returning to the heavens above Mt. Fuji.

This tradition of feminine association was combined with the particular symbolic appeal of Konohana Sakuya Hime as a woman who had survived childbirth in fire and hence could protect from the volcanic flames of the natural mountain. Her image as a flowering princess may have further been linked to the use of blossoms for crop divination, hence as a prayer for good crops among the farmers around the foot of the mountain who came to set up shrines to her (Ishigami 1985:1145). And most important, of course, she was beautiful—like the mountain itself.

In the Edo period, Konohana Sakuya Hime came to be one of the central images worshipped by the Fujikō cult, and it was perhaps through the influence of such believers that the goddess was widely revered in late Edo. In Hokusai's view here, however, there is little that would help identify her as specifically as Konohana Sakuya Hime; she is simply a generic Shintō deity. The image does serve, however, to begin the volume on a note of divine feminine beauty that is central to the Japanese conception of Mt. Fuji.

🐦 2. The Appearance of Mt. Fuji in the Fifth Year of Kōrei
(Kōrei gonen Fujimine shutsugen)

By the tenth century there had emerged the story that Lake Biwa and Mt. Fuji had been formed si-multaneously, the earth from the one being used to create the mound of the other. One cynical modern scholar has calculated that the mass of Mt. Fuji is in fact thirty-seven times that of Lake Biwa, the largest lake in Japan (Starr 1924:7), but this scarcely diminishes the appeal of the legend.

An exact date for this momentous event was even specified: the Fifth Year of the reign of the seventh emperor Kōrei, corresponding in the traditional account to 286 B.C.. Hokusai here wittily emphasizes the alleged historicity of the event, as two government officials to the left, seated on campstools with four attendants behind, witness the pristine mountain, its skirt shaded in a delicate gray and its summit bursting through the top frame of the page. To the right, a group of villagers make a careful record of the event. All eyes are on the mountain itself in a powerful depiction of focused attention— except, it seems, for the man pointing and the scribe following his gesture. I suspect this aversion of glance (seen also in No. 47) is a deliberate device to heighten the tension; one wonders what they are looking at, if not the mountain. The drama is sustained in other small details, such as the astonishing gestures of the two officials' hands.

🐦 3. En no Gyōja Opens Mt. Fuji
(En no Ubasoku Fugaku sōsō)

E no Ozunu was a historical figure of the seventh century whom time transformed into the legendary En no Gyōja, a practitioner (gyōja) of Buddhist austerities on high mountains who came to be known as the founder of Shugendō, a religion of mountain ascetics. En no Gyōja (also known, as in the title here, as an *ubasoku*, or unofficial priest) became the first man to climb Mt. Fuji, as related in the *Nihon ryōiki* of a century later. This occured during his exile to the island of Ōshima, fifty miles southeast of the mountain, in the years 699-701. During the day he remained on the island as ordered, but by night he flew across the waters to ascend Fuji and meditate there. Hence the title uses the term *sōsō*, the "founding" of a temple, to suggest that En no Gyōja "opened" the mountain to religious practice.

Hokusai has shown this primal mountain ascetic posed on the edge of what we take to be the crater of Fuji, his high clogs set to one side as he assumes the cross-legged Lotus position of meditation on a straw mat. His clothing (said to be made of vines) and tasseled rosary are whipped by the furious winds, but he is like a rock, posed against the axis of his black-tipped staff.

His hands assume what would appear to be esoteric Buddhist signs for the sword of Fudō (Matsuda 1969:35-36). Peering into the roiling gray clouds belching forth from the crater beyond, we can make out the objects of this powerful exorcising gesture, the faces of countless malicious spirits (oni) who tempt and threaten him. At least thirteen separate faces can be distinguished, one of them (just above and to the left of the rosary tassel) holding a staff which echoes that of the holy man himself.

En no Gyōja was described in the Nihon ryōiki as having a "mysterious magical power" that enabled him to "employ spirits and kami at his command" (Nakamura 1973:141); and in earlier depictions by Hokusai himself (Hokusai Manga, vol. X, and Hokusai gashiki, both 1819), he is shown with two particular spirits, Zenki and Goki, whom he has tamed into personal attendants. These earlier images, however, show a doddering old man and convey none of the tremendous power that we feel here.

4. Fuji under Clear Skies
(Kaisei no Fuji)

Following three views that established the form of Fuji in myth, history, and legend, we now break through to the mountain itself in its majestic physical presence. We look over a body of water below—perhaps Sagami Bay, but it does not matter. To the left are the tiny forms of boats bobbing in the winter swell, and in the sky above, three lonely birds. The foothills are shown in the "moss dot" style of which Hokusai was fond, rising to rocky crests that ring the white slopes of Fuji. High cirrus clouds line the sky, remnants of the storm that has passed and left the clear weather of the title.

This view is inevitably compared with its counterpart in the Thirty-Six Views of Mt. Fuji, the print entitled "Clear Skies with a Breeze from the South" (Gaifū kaisei) but generally known by its nickname "Red Fuji." It is a revealing comparison, for it shows that Hokusai has compensated for the color that he used so expressively in "Red Fuji" by adding more elaborate detail to draw our interest. He has provided the tiny boats and birds, for

example, where there were none in "Red Fuji." He has turned a spring or summer scene into a winter one, so as to put the whites and grays of monochrome printing to best advantage. The result is a wholly different aesthetic experience.

5. The Opening of Fuji
(Fuji no yamaaki)

6. Sliding Down
(Suberi)

Now we zoom in from broad expanse to close-up for a succession of two views of pilgrims on the face of the mountain itself. These are best seen and understood as a pair: the slow and arduous climb on the right, and the equally quick and rhythmic descent on the left.

These are among several views (see also Nos. 46 and 76) that depict the practice of climbing Fuji by the believers of the Fujikō religion. All of them strongly suggest that Hokusai never climbed the mountain himself, for they are unrealistic to the point of abstraction. To the right, for example, the pilgrims file through a narrow passage of a sort not found on the wide, open slopes of the normal climbing routes; and the one charming detail that saves the view from total abstraction—the pilgrim blowing on a conch-shell horn below—is probably wrong: to the best of my knowledge, this sort of horn was used by Shugendō ascetics, but not by Fujikō believers. Finally, the title of the print is written with characters that should properly be read "yamaaki," but the proper term for the annual "opening" of the mountain to climbers on the first day of the Sixth Month was (and remains, although changed to July 1 in the Western calendar) "yamabiraki."

The view of the descent to the left shows, as the title indicates, a "sliding" through the soft volcanic sand that accumulates here and there on the face of the mountain. This was in fact a common mode of quick descent—and quite the thrilling one that Hokusai suggests here—which remained possible on the Yoshida trail until an accident on August 14, 1980, when twelve people were killed in a rockslide along the subashiri ("sand run"), resulting in its closing and forcing all climbers since to make their way painfully down one of the much rougher bulldozer trails.

7. The Appearance of Hōeizan
(Hōeizan shutsugen)

In the winter of late 1707, in the dark of night, the great volcano suddenly exploded in what was one of the largest of the twenty-odd eruptions recorded in historical times. The encyclopedia *Wakan sansai zue*, the most likely source for Hokusai's own knowledge of an event that occured fifty-three years before his birth, reports that the earth shook under the explosion, as cinders and ashes were spewed forth over an area some seventy miles in radius. The volcano calmed but then on the third and fourth days erupted again in full fury, showering rocks and stones from the crater.

Hokusai has here let his imagination run free, in what is less specifically an image of volcanic eruption than an utter demolition of the everyday world. Fragments of rock shower down from the blackness above and beyond, but the inner force seems to come from somewhere below, hurling into the air three figures and a virtual catalog of the tools of daily life: jars, buckets, doors, axes, clothing, tiles. Below, several men and one horse lie pinned under the debris, while others frantically struggle to pull or carry their families to safety. It is an image of chaos as thorough as the image of peaceful stillness that we saw two pages before.

8. Part II of the Same
(Sono ni)

The great eruption of 1707 that we just saw was not from the central crater of Mt. Fuji but through a lateral vent on the southeast face of the mountain. This left a new crater formation projecting from the side, which within a year was christened Hōeizan ("Mt. Hōei"), after its occurence in the fourth year of the Hōei period. In this view, we can see the new lump to the right, which means we must be looking from the south. In the foreground is a familiar array of Hokusai types, all looking and laughing. The laugh is presumably on the second man from the left, from the side of whose face protrudes a huge round growth. Dickins in his 1880 commentary, incidentally, insisted that the man in question "is not afflicted with a tumor on the neck; what appears such is the bottom of an upturned gourd."

This view is in all likelihood both the first and last time that Hokusai ever drew this blemish on the

perfect form of Fuji. The Hōei eruption itself was also the last such event, for at least the foreseeable future: Mt. Fuji is still formally classified as active, but the chance of a major eruption is presently slim.

9. Fuji in the Mists
(Muchū no Fuji)

The versatile printing technique here creates two worlds juxtaposed. In the foreground, crisply carved in fine detail, a nonchalant procession of childlike figures mounts through the picture frame and exits above right along a rocky ridge. In the gray distance beyond to the left, we can make out a broader landscape of boats moving along the water below; further on is an inlet and a tiny village. Above, rows of trees, and in the distance, the perfect form of the mountain. These subtle effects were achieved through the printing of two different blocks of gray, each carefully shaded.

10. Fuji in the Mountains
(Sanchū no Fuji)

In his constant effort to show Fuji from every angle, Hokusai occasionally offered depictions from the mountains inland rather than from the more familiar vantage points in Edo and along the coast highway. This is one such, in a composition dominated by a massive old tree in the hollow of which women can be seen collecting mushrooms. It is almost a game to pick out the various bodies—five in all. To the lower left, two hunters load their guns.

11. Fuji over a Willow Bank
(Ryūtō no Fuji)

This is a finely composed scene of figures distributed over a willow-planted embankment, which was probably constructed to create the pond below. Travelers enter the picture from lower left and lower right, by roads that join at a stone marker. The characters engraved on the marker are frustratingly difficult to make out, but perhaps intentionally so, to give the universal sense of a generic place—it could be anywhere around the mountain. Travelers move along the embankment, two pausing for a pipe in full view of the mountain, while others proceed along the lower side, wholly indifferent.

12. Fuji at Tanabata
(Tanabata no Fuji)

This view is from Edo, a city in which the festive decorations for the festival of Tanabata on the seventh day of the Seventh Month had become a matter of ostentatious display by the 1830s. As we see here, long bamboo poles were lashed to drying stands atop houses, and to them were tied in turn fresh branches of bamboo. Among these branches were then strung paper sheets, some square and some oblong, on which poems were inscribed as offerings to the two lovers, the Cowherd and the Weaving Girl, who according to ancient Chinese legend were able to cross the Milky Way on this one day each year. Here the Tanabata decorations provide Hokusai with the material for the first in a number of similar witty compositions, in which we see the form of Fuji through an enlarged close-up object. He has here shown the details of the construction of the poles in fine detail, down to the individual strands of knots.

13. Sodegaura
(Sodegaura)

This is the first of three curious anomalies, single-page landscapes in which the name "Fuji" is missing from the title, although the mountain itself of course clearly appears in view. This one and the next also offer a problem of exact placement even though they have titles (the first such in the series) with proper place names.

In this particular instance, the actual place cannot be in doubt, since Hokusai had depicted it a number of times before, most recently in "Shichirigahama in Sagami Province" in the *Thirty-Six Views of Mt. Fuji*. There one sees the same rocky outcropping with Fuji rising to the right, the same cave cut into the rock below with two images, the same village nestled to the right, and the same islands extending to the left. Shichirigahama ("Seven Mile Beach") is a stretch of shore located between Enoshima (the island off to the left) and Kamakura. The place is even more specifically identified in a surimono by Hokusai, datable to 1821 (reproduced in Narazaki 1943, fig. 167). It again shows exactly the same scene, with the notation "A distant view of Koshigoe from Shichirigahama." Koshigoe is the area just east of the entrance to Enoshima, and the

promontory here is probably that known as Cape Koyurugi.

The confusion arises from the title "Sodegaura," which properly describes not Shichirigahama, but a stretch of shoreline lying further west, beyond Enoshima, between Hiratsuka and Odawara. Why did Hokusai alter the place name for a view he had drawn just two or three years previously? We can only guess at what was happening: whether Hokusai was losing his memory or simply didn't care —perhaps he was intentionally obscuring the specificity of the view.

An alternate theory, proposed by Nagata Seiji (1972:23–24), holds that this is a different Sodegaura, on the Chiba Peninsula, now a stop on the Sōbu Main Line. I find this untenable.

14. Fujimigahara in Owari Province
(Bishū Fujimigahara)

This view again recalls a parallel from the *Thirty-Six Views of Mt. Fuji*, in this instance "Umezawa in Sagami Province," in which a group of cranes is likewise placed in the foreground— although the effect here is more crowded, less elegant. The title here, however, indicates not Umezawa (which by curious coincidence is actually located along the coast of Sodegaura, the title of the previous print), but rather Fujimigahara (which by further coincidence happens to be the title of a completely different print in the *Thirty-Six Views*, the famous one of Fuji as seen through the bottom of a huge bucket under construction).

The exact identity of Fujimigahara long remained a mystery until Kobayashi Tadashi (1976:109) identified the place as part of the city of Nagoya, where a famous brothel had flourished briefly in the early eighteenth century. Thereafter, however, it seems to have reverted to its literal name, "Fuji View Plain." The landscape here does in fact support this theory, in the very small size of Fuji, since Fujimigahara ties with Nikkō (No. 63) as the most distant point from which the mountain is viewed in this series (with the exception of the imaginary Orankai in No. 73).

15. Mountains Upon Mountains
(Yama mata yama)

It would be fruitless to search for any particular locale here, for Hokusai is simply expressing the literal meaning of the title, with the mountain to end all mountains surpassing the lesser ones both in form and in height. The sense of recession by the reduction of size with distance is a technique Hokusai learned from the West, which sets this apart from traditional Chinese and Japanese landscape method. The title also recalls an illustrated poetry album of the same name that Hokusai designed in 1804; there, however, it indicated a series of views in the hilly area surrounding Edo rather than a single image of "mountains on mountains" as here.

16. Ōmori
(Ōmori)

This conventional view overlooks Edo Bay off Ōmori, outside the southern limits of the city, where seaweed (*nori*, the kind used to wrap sushi) was cultivated on the bamboo stakes that we see projecting from the water. This is one of the few instances in which Hokusai depicts a specific Edo place in its characteristic garb—although with no great interest or even accuracy (since neither of the two boats shown here were the kind used to harvest the seaweed).

17. Fuji from a Cave
(Dōchū no Fuji)

Two woodcutters rest their bundles of kindling by the entrance to a cave that frames our view.

18. Fuji from a Pine Mountain
(Matsuyama no Fuji)

The name Matsuyama could be a proper name, but here it is surely generic—a view through any of the pine forests to be found on the skirts of Mt. Fuji. Local people in diverse attire emerge from the valley below and move into the pines to gather the prize *matsutake* mushrooms, of which we get a glimpse in the basket on the head of the man below, left of center.

19. Fuji through Smoke
(Enchū no Fuji)

In a conceit that verges on the precious, we see travelers on the left kindling a fire with the autumn foliage that floats through the air to the right. The smoke drifts off in a gracefully printed wave of gray, finally obscuring all but two remaining patches of white at Fuji's crest and skirt. The decorative elegance of the horse and mountain to the right stands in contrast to the tense melange of detail on the left.

Above the three travelers stands a Kōshin shrine. Derived from Chinese Taoist practice, this cult was rooted in the belief that the Day of the Monkey, in a calendrical combination (*kōshin*) which recurs once every sixty days, was a time of danger that called for protective measures. In the Japanese version, both the danger and the protection were afforded by the Kōshin god, whose name "Shōmen Kongō" is here inscribed on a rock within a circle. This god, in original Buddhist iconography a ferocious "blue-faced" (*shōmen*) deity, came also to be identified, by way of the Day of the Monkey, with the image of the Three Monkeys ("See No Evil, Speak No Evil, Hear No Evil") that we can see shown in the square section directly below. Sometimes the Monkeys were seen as the god itself, sometimes as messengers of the god. It was one of the many popular beliefs in Tokugawa Japan that involved an intricate and not always consistent interweaving of Taoist, Buddhist, and indigenous belief.

The appearance of the Kōshin images here reveals a further link with the god of travel, Sarutahiko, whose name contains the word "monkey." Hence Kōshin shrines ended up guarding travelers such as the ones here, who carelessly cloud the face of Fuji with their autumn bonfire.

20. Fuji on the Face of a Paddy
(Tanomo no Fuji)

This view involves the only literary conceit in the entire *One Hundred Hundred Views of Mt. Fuji*. As Suzuki Jūzō appears to have been the first to notice, the title recalls the stock poetic phrase "tanomu no kari," a word play (Kakekotoba) which links the image of geese (*kari*) descending to the "face of a rice paddy" (*tanomo*) with the verb "to beseech" (*tanomu*). A classic instance appears in the tenth chapter of *Tales of Ise*.

21. Fuji with Rafts in the Rushes
(Rochū ikada no Fuji)

This view is a consistent favorite with modern Japanese commentators, perhaps because it has a hint of sentimentality that is rare in Hokusai. Particularly fetching is the child—exquisitely perched at the end of a lashed bundle of lumber, ever so gracefully bending them as he hangs out over the water—peering at the sacred mountain in the distance. To the right, one casual fisherman baits his hook, while the other tosses his into the river. Narazaki Muneshige, peering through the twentieth-century lens worn by so many modern Japanese scholars of ukiyo-e, assumed that these fishermen were on an outing from Edo and saw in them the blissful escape to "nature" of urban man, "besmirched by the yellow dust, aimlessly led astray by the red lights" (Narazaki 1971:104). Hokusai and his contemporary viewers would have been bemused.

In mid-river are the rafts of the title, logs lashed together for transportation from the forests downriver to port. Five are shown here, dissolving into the distance on the right against a vastly enlarged reedbed in a way that shows how Hokusai knowingly violated perspective in favor of design and pattern.

22. Fuji in a Winter Wind
(Kogarashi no Fuji)

A chill wind whips across the fields of winter crops and threatens to tear away the elaborate system of defense against birds—strings of wooden noisemakers and a raised guard-hut for tugging them on windless days. But today the system of defense is itself defenseless, as are the three figures who struggle against the wind below. The sawed-off stump of a huge tree to the right adds a powerful sense of chill and a deeper meaning to the title kogarashi, literally a "witherer of trees." Above it all, unperturbed, the Mountain.

23. Fuji on New Year's Day
(Gantan no Fuji)

Hokusai has here skillfully crowded into one page a whole range of New Year's Day performers. The lack of any surrounding buildings suggests that we may be traveling along a highway in the country, but in fact such an assembly could be found only in the middle of Edo. To the left is the familiar New Year's decoration of East Japan, the kadomatsu or "gate pine," which is set before the entrance to every house of consequence. Stakes were driven into the

ground to form a round enclosure, bound with rope, into which were packed branches of pine, and from the center a post to which branches of bamboo were lashed. The one we see here suggests a large mansion, probably a daimyo estate. Against it leans a kite, a traditional New Year's pastime; it bears the character fu, "prosperity," often used to write "Fuji."

Along the street move entertainers of all sorts. In the very center, a manzai performer in elaborate courtly robes is followed by his assistant in a matching pattern with the crest of the number three (a mark of unknown significance that appears on numerous occasions in this work; see also Nos. 8, 19, 35, 48). This pair will be making the round of samurai residences, performing celebratory chants and dances for the eternal prosperity of the families. Directly behind the assistant is a street minstrel, dressed in formal kamishimo attire; the smaller figure ahead of him is probably his assistant.

Off to the left, mostly hidden by the pine branches, we can spot the hat above and clogs below of a type of female performer known as tori-oi, who to the accompaniment of shamisen would sing auspicious songs. On New Year's Day alone, they wore this type of straw hat pulled forward and tied under the chin to hide the face. Look then just to the right of the straw hat, and you can make out the furry head and one tiny ear of a monkey, whose trainer holds the long pole with a cross and loop on which his pet will perform. The geometry of the monkey's tiny stage is harmonized with the geometry of the mountain.

Of the remaining figures, one shoulders a large box, probably a samurai retainer delivering New Year's gifts, while on the far right we make out a head below a huge pack marked on-wataboshi, a cotton cap of the sort that the bearer seems to be wearing. There is record of a fifteenth-century poem in which a cloud over Fuji is likened to precisely such a cap (Tyler 1981:145). It is doubtful that Hokusai knew the reference but likely that some parallel with the "white cap" of Fuji above is intended.

24. Fuji from Edo
(Edo no Fuji)

In this witty conception, the city of Edo is symbolized by a tile castle-roof ornament known as shachihoko ("dolphin spear"), representing an imaginary creature with the head of a dragon and arching tail of a fish. Since both dragons and fish live in water, the *shachihoko* attached to both ends of a ridgepole were believed to protect the building below from fire. Beyond this, however, the gilded *shachihoko* of Edo Castle had taken on a specific symbolism in the boast of the Edokko ("child of Edo," akin to London's Cockney) that he "took his first bath in water from the aqueduct, and peered through his garrett window at the gold *shachihoko*" (from a 1794 novelette by Santō Kyōden, cited in Nishiyama 1973:17), a mark of pride in a city assured of a constant water supply and looked over by the great castle of the shogun.

Hokusai goes one step further, however, in perching a plump little shrike at the tip of the monster's tail, its relaxed posture joining with that of Fuji in neat counterpoise to the entrapped fury of the monster below.

🐦 25. Fuji as a Mirror Stand
(Kyōdai Fuji)

From the area around Edo, the sun could in fact be seen setting in this way in the early fall, directly behind Mt. Fuji and casting off rays that recall to modern eyes the design of the Japanese naval ensign. Here, however, the image offered by the title is that of a Fuji as mirror-stand, surmounted by the sun as mirror. The sun's rays are shown with such delicacy (unlike later editions, where they dominate the scene) that we are rather drawn into the charming foreground scene, in which two fishermen push their boat under a low plank bridge.

Crossing the bridge is a fellow fisherman who has packed up for the day and is heading home with a package of food and a bottle of sake balanced on his oar and his dog curiously sniffing the contents of his basket. The scene reeks of humanity—literally so if Dickins were right in his assertion that the two large buckets to be left are filled with nightsoil. In fact, they are surely tubs for drying salt, as seen also in No. 57. This suggests that the place may be around Gyōtoku or Kisarazu on Edo Bay, both known for the making of salt.

🐦 26. Fuji from Behind
(Ura Fuji)

The sense of being "behind" Fuji, probably in the mountains of Kai Province, is emphasized by the

dark, irregular crest of the mountain, almost eclipsed by a nearby peak. But as in all of this series of six two-page spreads that conclude Volume I, we are offered a detailed foreground scene of daily human activity. Here we have a revealing depiction of the variety of ways in which a family in the hills might make a living. The tobacco leaves hung to dry on the rack to the left represent a valuable cash crop, while the woman on the right seems to be laying thread from her basket around a frame, perhaps for dying. In the left foreground, we see the careful cleaning of the horse who will carry these goods to market. As the man scrubs the rump of the beast over a wooden tub, a woman arranges the saddle while a tiny child peers playfully through a bucket handle.

🐦 27. Fuji with a Hat
(Kasa Fuji)

The "hat cloud" (*kasagumo*) that Mt. Fuji wears here is the term used by meteorologists today to describe the phenomenon by which warm air is driven up along the face of the mountain, condensing into a cloud of vapor at the peak. Although found on other mountains, the hat clouds of Fuji are particularly famous, warranting fully twelve photographs in one modern geographical compendium about the mountain (Takeda 1931:265-71).

Below, a diverse assortment of country folk is fording a broad river, all with a burden—a "cap," if you will—of some sort. Two guide oxen with loads of poles, while others carry a spinning wheel, a hoe, baskets, and so forth. The man to the right is an itinerant performer of the lion dance, his costume on his back.

🐦 28. Fuji with a Belt
(Untai no Fuji)

The title again indicates one of the many unusual cloud patterns caused by the massive mountain, in this case an encircling "belt" of vapor. And again, Hokusai offers a richly detailed foreground scene. We seem to be fairly high, near a fast mountain stream that drives the gristmill to the left, into which men carry sacks of grain. In the road, a team of three coolies bear a huge box under the guard of two samurai (the far one visible only in legs and hat). The rhythm of their jogging is set against the slow progress of the ox crossing the narrow bridge to the right, its passenger (perhaps a priest or doctor) gazing in utter detachment at the form of Fuji.

❦ 29. Fuji through Flowers
(Kakan no Fuji)

It requires close inspection to catch the subtle quality of the cherry blossoms printed in gray outline, like so many tiny puffs of cotton that combine into larger cloudlike clumps to frame the mountain. Blossom-viewing revelers to the left have set up their screen and laid out their mat for a day of eating, drinking, and dancing. Two of the men are singing and gesturing to the shamisen accompaniment of a geisha, while the third seems to be reaching out for more sake from the servant. In the foreground is a curious sort of hoist arrangement by which a basket of boxed food is pulled down along a rope. Perhaps the food was prepared in the restaurant above and is being sent down to the detached building below for distribution to customers in the garden. Both Dickins and Suzuki locate this scene in Edo: the one in Mukōjima, and the other at Asukayama. Hokusai had probably encountered such a food-hoist somewhere, but I doubt that the view can be identified as any particular place.

❦ 30. Fuji in a Good Harvest
(Hōsaku no Fuji)

The ripening grain extends as far as the eye can see, leading in one direction towards the sacred peak of Fuji, and in the other up through terraced paddies to a tiny village shrine that overlooks and protects the fields. A characteristic procession of humanity makes its way along the ground below, with a special accent added by the curious costume of the vender of "Korea Candy" (chōsen ame), a product of Kumamoto Prefecture made from sweetened sticky rice and said to have originated in Korea; the hat is supposedly Korean costume (see No. 68). The packhorses to the right wear blankets with various characters for "good luck" (shiawase-yoshi, daikichi), an old tradition that was supposed to protect the riders and which gave the term "good-luck horse" (shiawase-uma) as a synonym for packhorse. The markings appear also in Nos. 11 and 26, but Hokusai has doubtless emphasized them here to accent the auspicious meaning of the view as a whole.

❦ 31. Fuji Bountiful
(Senkin no Fuji)

The idea of bounty is carried over from the previous view to create this fitting conclusion to the first volume of One Hundred Views of Mt. Fuji—although there is a certain irony that this volume appeared just as East Japan was on the brink of disastrous famine. Two giant stacks of rice bales, each protected with a strip of straw mat, echo the distant form of the mountain itself as sparrows chirp and flit in the winter air in search of spare grains to eat. The title senkin literally means "a thousand pieces of gold" and, by extension, a priceless bounty. The theme is further reinforced by the use of the characters "prosperous gentlemen" to write the word "Fuji" in the title; this is the only view in the entire work in which these characters are used. Although this in fact has always been the most common way of writing "Fuji," Hokusai preferred the combination "not two," that is, "peerless."

❦ Colophon to Volume I

The first column, on the right, is Hokusai's signature. The five characters at the top give his age, "Seventy-five Years," while the next ones below to the right announce that his name has "Changed from 'Iitsu the Former Hokusai'" (Saki no Hokusai Iitsu aratamete). Then in large characters, the new name: "Gakyō Rōjin Manji." The seal below, printed in red in the original, shows the form of Fuji over the I Ching trigram for "Lake."

In the second column appears the famous postscript by Hokusai that is quoted in the Introduction (p. 7); and in the following column, the signature of the carver Egawa Tomekichi (with the seal of his formal name, Gojōtei).

There then follows a list of titles presumably offered by the publisher, first the One Hundred Views of Mt. Fuji itself, indicating the first volume as "already published" and the remaining two as "soon to be published." Each of the remaining eleven titles, all "soon to be published," includes the character "one hundred": One Hundred Unusual Flowers; One Hundred Quick Comic Sketches; One Hundred Views of Famous Bridges; One Hundred Magicians; Long Life and Prosperity One Hundred-Fold; One Hundred Views of Fishermen; One Hundred Views Beneath the Moon; One Hundred Views of Farmers; One Hundred Pictures Drawn Freehand:

Circles and Squares, Long and Short; *One Hundred Horses*; *One Hundred Oxen*; *One Hundred Birds*; *One Hundred Beasts*.

The final column on the second page of the colophon gives the date of publication, "Third Month, Spring, Tempō 5 [1834]," and a list of four booksellers: Eirakuya Tōshirō [Tōhekidō] of Nagoya, Kadomaruya Jinsuke [Shūseikaku] of Kōjimachi 4-chōme in Edo, Nishimura Yohachi [Eijudō] of Bakuro-chō 2-chōme in Edo, and Nishimura Yūzō [Seirindō], also of Bakuro-chō 2-chōme. The last of these was the primary publisher (as confirmed by the inside front cover); the others were co-distributors who may also have helped with the financing.

Volume II

❦ *Title Page*   (Inside Front Cover)

The inscriptions here remain the same as in Volume I; but the style of calligraphy has changed from cursive to a more formal script, and the border pattern of eggplant has been replaced by a witty design of stylized clouds above, sea below, and pines to either side—all elements that frequently appear framing Fuji in the actual views.

❦ *Preface to Volume II*

The seal in the margin to the upper right indicates that this volume was once in the collection of Hayashi Tadamasa (1853–1906), the famous Japanese art dealer who played a key role in introducing ukiyo-e prints to France in the late nineteenth century and who was the major informant for Edmond de Goncourt in preparing his biography of Hokusai (de Goncourt 1896).

The translation of the preface is as follows: The mountain of Fuji, its form like a carved jewel, its color that of burnished silver, having neither front nor back, neither sticking out nor leaning over, on all sides it is as flawless as a lotus blossom rising from the pond, as it straddles the summits of all the many other peaks. Thus it dominates the entire realm. The red of sunrise sparkles on its whiteness, and with the setting sun it takes on hues of blue and green. Morning and evening the color varies, near

and far the prospect differs. It changes in endless ways, through spring haze and in autumn wind, under clouds or mist, in light and dark. Old Hokusai has drawn one hundred views, and the perfection of his craft makes them come to life. In these pictures we bear witness to the wondrous sight of changes one hundred-fold.

> First Month, Tenpō 6 [1835]
> Rozan Kō [Takashi?]
> [Seals: Shuseian and Risei (Satoi?)]

Note: Kojima (1931:84) identifies the author of this preface, presumably from the seals, as "Satoi Morifumi." "Morifumi" appears to be his reading of the first two characters of the upper seal, but only the first is plausible, while "Satoi" is probably rather read "Risei" and represents, like Rozan, an art-name (*gō*) rather than a family name. Kō (Takashi?) is probably the personal name. Whatever his name, we have no idea who he was.

❦ 32.   Well-Cleaning Fuji
(Ido-sarae no Fuji)

Although the frame cuts off the surrounding locale, we must be in the middle of the city of Edo, where wells were fed not by groundwater but by a complex system of underground wooden pipes. Such wells were periodically cleaned by shutting off the inlet, then bailing out the water that remained. This shows how it seems to have been done, by pairs of workmen: one standing astride the well to manipulate the bucket, and the other supplying the hoisting power by way of a ladder-supported post with pulley. Hokusai carefully shows the way in which the ladders are lashed to the post, but his greater delight is in the complex geometrical variation of form that the device allows. In addition to the triangular forms that echo the shape of the mountain, there is a complex play of curves, with the body of the workman arched in a near-perfect semicircle.

❦ 33.   Fuji and Yatsugatake in Shinshū
(Shinshū Yatsugatake no Fuji)

Yatsugatake is, as its name indicates, a volcanic cluster of "Eight Peaks" (the highest being 9,509 feet) lying some fifty miles northwest of Mt. Fuji, across the Kōfu Basin. Like Fuji itself, it is part of the broad volcanic belt that cuts through central Japan. Almost all of the craters of Yatsugatake, however, have been eroded into a rough and jagged outline that contrasts with the pure form of Fuji. Hokusai has clearly expressed this contrast in the tiny scene to the upper left, where Yatsugatake is seen just below Mt. Fuji and a bit to the left; it appears that Hokusai has carefully drawn eight separate peaks, although all eight can never in fact be seen from one place. This view of the two peaks side by side is prefigured in an earlier design of the same title in *Contemporary Patterns for Combs and Pipes* (Imayō sekkin hinagata, II, 1823; see Nagata 1986:4.152).

The body of water in the foreground must be Lake Suwa, judging by the similarity of the skyline to that in "Lake Suwa in Shinshū" in the *Thirty-Six Views of Mt. Fuji*. In that view, Yatsugatake is shown higher than Fuji, as it would in fact appear from Lake Suwa; Hokusai had, however, previously shown Fuji as higher in a view of "Crossing the Ice on Lake Suwa in Shinshū" in *Hokusai Manga*, vol. X (1819). But how can we explain the contradiction between the calm expanse of the lake beyond and the rough waters against which fishermen battle in their log boat below? It was this foreground view that led Suzuki Jūzō to conclude that the place must be an imagined scene from some river, possibly the Chikuma River.

The foreground scene is better understood, however, by looking at another of the *Thirty-six Views of Mt. Fuji*, that of "Kajikizawa in Kai Province," in which a single fisherman stands on a rocky outcropping above the surging rapids of the Fuji River—a figure that is almost precisely replicated by the one in the bow of the boat we see here. The only answer can be that Hokusai has freely joined two wholly different scenes from previous depictions of Fuji in order to create a new composite that is in the end beyond any particular location. The inconsistency of place is resolved into a unity of compositional meaning by which the tiny but constant form of Fuji serves as counterpoint to the swirling waters below, timelessness set against constant change.

❦ 34. Fuji in a Bamboo Grove
(Chikurin no Fuji)

The superb decorative beauty of this composition makes it one of the most favored in the entire series. It is a rather more complex composition than it first appears, for in a sense it shows the interweaving of *two* bamboo groves—one of mature trees in the foreground and one of new shoots forcing their way up-

ward from behind, still covered with their protective sheaths. The pliant grace of the older trees is thus nicely complemented by the assertive vigor of the young shoots, which can in fact grow at the rate of as much as one foot per day. All is finely balanced against the form of Fuji beyond, the white peak emerging from a wash of pale gray.

❦ 35. Fuji over a Bank
(Tsutsumigoshi no Fuji)

A quality of mystery pervades this print. In the lower left is the basket and fishing net of a person unseen. The curve of the grass on the shore below seems to combine with the log bridge and its mooring to create the phantom image of a boat. The figure crossing the bridge, balancing a teapot on a hoe, is a bafflingly exact copy of a woman crossing another sort of bridge in "Nakahara" from the *Thirty-six Views of Mt. Fuji* (Kondo 1966:fig. 26). The other figures also seem from separate worlds, distracted. The form of Fuji is rough, blackened below. Two trees emerge from the otherwise barren bank, one breaking through the frame. Perhaps I am reading too much into an innocent rural scene, which was after all one of two views from this series (with No. 53) that de Chassiron (1861) chose as examples of illustration from popular Japanese books; he entitled this one "Customs of the Country" (Moeurs de la campagne). I nevertheless find it an unsettling landscape.

❦ 36. Fuji and Ascending Dragon
(Tōryū no Fuji)

From the dark depths, the dragon climbs heavenward, casting off curly waves that suggest his watery lair. The dragon was said to reside in his lake for one thousand years practicing austerities before rising heavenward in what became a standard metaphor for success; one source says that the image of the dragon in clouds across Fuji was specifically an "emblem of worldly success" (Joly 1967:33). This is one of two views (with No. 52) in the series in which a separate block of black (rather than gray) was used for background gradation, in both instances to fine effect.

Hokusai's preliminary sketch for this print, as for several others in the series, survives and offers precious evidence for the way in which the artist first conceptualized his views. See Hillier (1980:222–23) for the first sketches of this and Nos. 52 and 57.

37. Fuji on the Swell
(Uneri Fuji)

This view might be understood as a sequel to the famous "Great Wave" in the *Thirty-six Views of Mt. Fuji*, in which three boats of the sort we see here—oar-driven *oshiokuri-bune* designed for the swift delivery of fresh fish to market—face into the fury of a giant wave. Now, the storm has subsided and the boatmen are safe but exhausted. The great cresting waves have ceased, but in their place the rhythmic up-and-down of the swell makes it impossible to relax. The six oarsmen (two fewer than in the "Great Wave" boats) continue to struggle against the sea, huddled in united effort.

And then there magically appears the image of the mountain on the waves, which distort its shape with their restless action. Is it a wave itself or a reflection of Fuji? Is it seen by the boatmen or by us? Is it real? It seems best not to ponder the precise optics of the image, which were surely worked out in Hokusai's own imagination rather than in visual experience, and to accept it as a sign that the mountain is omnipresent for the boatmen, an assurance that they will return safely.

38. Fuji of the Dyers' Quarter
(Konya'chō no Fuji)

Through the long strips of cotton cloth that hang from a rooftop drying stand of a dyer in Edo, we make out the form of Fuji. It takes a second to realize that something is actually going on here: a long bamboo pole from an invisible hand below is lifting a wet piece of freshly-dyed cloth onto the end of one of the poles. (For what is in effect the missing bottom part of the scene here, see the view of a dyer's establishment in Hokusai's *Azuma asobi* of 1799.) This witty detail emphasizes the sense of a moment against the timelessness of the half-hidden mountain.

39. Fuji in a Winecup
(Haichū no Fuji)

The elaborate array of feathers overflowing from the fisherman's basket and curling around the tree is

the clue that Hokusai is here depicting the folk tale of Hagoromo, the "Feathered Robe." The tale has many variations throughout Japan, but the most famous is that which is set at Miho on Suruga Bay and which became widely known through the Nō play *Hagoromo*. The story begins when the fisherman Hakuryō arrives at the beach of Miho and discovers a beautiful feathered robe hanging from one of the pine trees for which the place was celebrated. He is pleased by his find and prepares to take the robe home: it is this moment which Hokusai depicts, as the fisherman celebrates by pouring some sake from his flask and is delighted to see the auspicious reflection of Fuji in the winecup.

In the Nō play, the angel (*tennyo*) who owns the robe appears and begs that Hakuryō give it back, which he finally agrees to do in return for the performance of a heavenly dance. (In the common folktale pattern, the fisherman first obliges the *tennyo* to marry him, but she later recovers the robe and returns to heaven.) The dance is performed, and the *tennyo* rises off into the sky, up to the peak of Fuji itself and on beyond into the mists of heaven. Hokusai's humorous depiction is much closer in spirit to the folktale than to the noble Nō play.

40. Fuji at Sea
(Kaijō no Fuji)

Here Hokusai once again presents the "Great Wave," a theme which he had shown many years before in "The Wave of Honmoku off Kanagawa" (one of his early Western-style prints of about 1805), and which he had redesigned most recently in the famous version from the *Thirty-six Views of Mt. Fuji*. Here, however, he changes the conception completely, most revealingly by reversing the direction of the wave. Since the Japanese eye moves across the composition from right to left, it here proceeds in company with the wave rather than in opposition to it. And rather than men struggling with nature, we now see nature in unison with nature, in the flock of plovers who seem to be cast off from the wave itself as bits of froth.

Hokusai had actually depicted the interplay of birds and wave a few years earlier, in a print of 1830 that shows not a broad landscape like this, but a close-up of four sparrows playing about the tip of a cresting wave (Hillier 1978:63, Yasuda 1971:140). Here he has taken this idea and merged it with the "Great Wave" to produce the most remarkable composition in the entire series.

41. Fuji from Susaki
(Susaki no Fuji)

The Susaki of the title must refer to the narrow spit of land (*susaki*) that lay at the mouth of the Sumida River in the Fukagawa district of Edo. At the neck of the strand was a famous Benten shrine, dedicated to the goddess who protects sources of water; the roof to the lower right must be that of the main shrine building. The black form of Fuji suggests that the time is dusk, ironic in view of the fame of Susaki Benten as a place to watch the sunrise. The whole image here is somehow detached and lonely, with a human presence visible only in the tiny heads hidden under the straw shelter on the boat.

42. Fuji in a Dream
(Yume no Fuji)

This disturbing image has its origins in a proverbial description of the three things that would bring good luck if seen (not necessarily in combination) in the first dream of the New Year: Mt. Fuji, a falcon, and an eggplant (*ichi Fuji, ni taka, san nasubi*). Why such an implausible combination? The three competing theories cited in *Nihon kokugo daijiten* offer insight into the witty mechanisms of Japanese proverb-making—or at least proverb-explaining. First, that it is a list of the most famous products of Suruga Province (now Shizuoka Prefecture); the falcon probably derives from the connection with the Suruga origins of the Tokugawa family, which was inordinately fond of hawking. Second, that it ranks the highest things in Suruga: Mt. Fuji obviously first, then Mt. Ashitaka (punning on *-taka* and *taka*, "falcon," and taking high to mean "expensive" in the case of the eggplant, which fetched high prices when it first appeared on the market). Third, that the words all have connotations of commercial profit: Fuji is high (that is, expensive), falcons seize [profit], and the work for eggplant (*nasu*) is a synonym for the verb that variously means accomplish, perform, give birth.

Hokusai doubtless intended to draw on the essentially auspicious quality of the proverb, but in the end produced an image that must reflect the disturbed recesses of his imagination. The falcon is shown attacking a pheasant, in a massive collision of feathers that almost defies our efforts to discern one bird from the other (although it can in fact be done—with effort). The final focus of the attack is

in the counterpoise of the two heads: the hawk with eye open wide, beak firmly shut in victory, and the pheasant with eye closed, mouth open in death. From behind the struggle emerges the gently curling pattern of eggplant leaves—one flower strangely detached to the right (and not looking at all like a real eggplant blossom), and four fruits blended into the jumbled composition.

Finally Fuji, Number One, delicately etched in the contour of the gray block, above and beyond the fantasy of the artist's contorted dream below.

43. "Three Whites" Fuji
(Sanpaku no Fuji)

The "Three Whites" constituted a set formula in Japanese painting in the Chinese manner, with inevitably auspicious overtones. The archetypal formula seems to have been snow plus bird (white heron or white falcon) plus flower (white plum or narcissus). Here Hokusai has replaced the flower with Fuji, set off against a heron on a snowy pine branch and a pattern of snowflakes falling through the gray sky.

44. The First Hanging Scroll
(Kakemono no hottan)

An old servant at an inn, duster stuck in sash, has taken off the paper shoji for cleaning and points out the fine view of Mt. Fuji to the visitor. The guest is astonished, dropping his pipe and tobacco jar and spreading his fingers in utter surprise—not at the view of Fuji, but at the impression that it is framed just like a hanging scroll, set off by the wall partitions above and below. This is the way, the title implies, the format of a hanging scroll was first discovered.

This is a simple-minded conceit, one might argue; yet it can also be understood as a searching query into the nature of pictures, a query that would be pressed to ironic extremes in certain of Magritte's twentieth-century images. Remember that Western linear perspective originated in the conception of a window through which the exterior world was viewed, and that Japanese artists like Hokusai had been much influenced by the idea of perspective and by the concept of pictures that present reality "as if before one's very eyes."

The meaning is enhanced by the Chinese poem on the wall to the upper right, inscribed in archaic seal script. It means something like "Flowers bloom and fall before my very eyes, clouds come and go above the mountain peak." I have not yet found the source of the poem but suspect that Hokusai intended to suggest another classical problem of pictures: how to capture change and movement on an unchanging surface. He himself has certainly managed to do it here by showing the dramatic reaction of a man confronted with the enduring question, what is a picture?

🦋 45. Fuji Through Pines
(Matsugoshi no Fuji)

We are reminded of the title page, in which pines similarly frame the mountain. The composition is of the near-far type normally reserved in this series for views from the city of Edo.

🦋 46. A Rock Shelter on Fuji
(Fuji no muro)

This is essentially a scaled-down version of what has been taken to be the concluding view of the *Thirty-six Views of Mt. Fuji*, "People Climbing the Mountain," showing a winding row of pilgrims making their way up to a cave filled with huddling forms. Here we move in closer, with two climbers below and ten sitting in the cave. As with Nos. 5–6, it seems clear that Hokusai had no actual experience of what it was like to climb Mt. Fuji. The shelters (*muro*) in which pilgrims rested on the way up were not caves of the sort shown here, but structures framed with timber and lined with rocks carefully sorted from the volcanic rubble. Even though it is Hokusai's fantasy, the view nevertheless conveys the sense of womblike security that these shelters doubtless offered the climbing pilgrims.

🦋 47. Drawing Fuji from Life
(Shashin no Fuji)

A painter, evidently a man of some distinction, has carefully laid his sword to one side and taken up his brushes. He sits, paper ready, peering intently at the nicely varied landscape before him; his gaze seems directed not at the mountain, but at the small shrine by a tree jutting out over the river. His three atten-

dants in matched attire prepare sake, open a bundle, and take out rolls of paper or silk for painting. A lone heron sits perched on a post above the artist, watching in unison.

Edmond de Goncourt was the first to propose, in 1896, that the artist shown here is Hokusai himself (de Goncourt 1896: 211). Japanese scholars have tended to deny the suggestion, on the grounds that an ordinary artist like Hokusai would never have been able to travel with three servants. Tsuji Nobuo sees the attendants as disciples rather than servants (a thin line in the Japanese teaching profession), but makes the more basic point that Hokusai has depicted not himself but rather an idealized pose that he himself would never have assumed, for he surely composed landscapes in his head and not from direct observation (Tsuji 1982: 143).

The more basic question, however, is exactly what the painter here is doing, or more concretely, what sort of image will appear on the blank sheet of paper in front of him? This is a tricky question to answer, and perhaps Hokusai intended it so. Take the word "*shashin*" of the title, for example. It literally means "copy the truth," which obviously can mean different things to different people, and in fact did so in Hokusai's time. When Shiba Kōkan used *shashin* in his famous *Discussion of Western Painting* in 1799, he was referring to realism in Western-style oil painting; it was for this reason that the word would later be used to translate "photograph." But when Hokusai himself used it in the title of his exquisite picture-book *Hokusai shashin gafu* in 1814, he certainly did not have Western realism in mind. The contents suggest, rather, a simplified style, with minimal detail, which seeks to "capture the idea" of an object rather than its literal appearance—in effect, the opposite of Kōkan's meaning.

In this view, however, the term *shashin* seems to indicate a related but still different sense, of drawing directly from life; Suzuki has suggested that the reading *shō–utsushi* would be more appropriate to express this meaning. It does not necessarily follow, however, that the picture which will appear on the blank paper below will be "realistic" in any Western sense. In the case of Hokusai, one would imagine, it is rather a matter of drawing *inspiration* from life. In the end, then, we cannot really predict the relationship between the keen gaze of the painter here and his brushes poised below. Given the ferment in thinking about this issue in late Tokugawa Japan, one can imagine quite a wide variety of responses.

48. Shichikyō ichiran no Fuji
(Fuji with Seven Bridges in One View)

Hokusai loved bridges and painted them endlessly. In particular, he designed in the early 1820s, an amazing large-size color print "One Hundred Bridges in a Single View" (Hyakkyō ichiran)—a title appearing not on the print but in an 1823 advertisement (see Nagata 1985:71)—depicting an intricate mountain landscape filled with bridges of every description, at least one hundred in all. Here he has reduced the number to a mere seven, but it is somewhat of a game to find them all. The most difficult one to spot is the very simple structure, apparently just a log or two, which lies to the far left, under the large arching bridge above. It is unclear why Hokusai chose the number seven; eight would have been more conventional. Perhaps he had in mind the form of Mt. Fuji itself as an eighth bridge; note how it is echoed in the two smaller bridges just below it to the right and left.

49. Fuji in the Mountains of Taisekiji Temple
(Taisekiji no sanchū no Fuji)

Taisekiji is today the main temple of the Nichiren Shōshū sect, best known for the strength of its lay organization, Sōka Gakkai. In Hokusai's day, however, it did not constitute a separate sect and was merely one of several major Nichiren temples in the Fuji area. It lies at the very base of Mt. Fuji, to the southwest, some four miles north of Fujinomiya. In this view, however, Hokusai simply indicates by the title that it is the mountains of Taisekiji; the temple itself is nowhere in sight. The center of attraction is the curious rock formation in the center, but it has been impossible to identify any such sight in the Taisekiji area.

Why did his choose this view? It is possible that he was inspired by one of the designs in Kawamura Minsetsu's *Hundred Fujis* of 1767, which has the identical title, although the composition is wholly different. Or perhaps there is some connection with Hokusai's own Nichiren faith. Whatever the connection with Taisekiji, Hokusai seems to have been interested in the more rugged form of the mountain peak as seen from this direction (although scarcely as rough as he shows it here); perhaps he was then inspired to devise a rock formation that echoes it.

50. Fuji in the Evening Sun at Shimadagahana
(Shimadagahana sekiyō Fuji)

This appealing scene is by far the most detailed depiction of the city of Edo to be found in the *One Hundred Views of Mt. Fuji*, but the exact location has been difficult to pin down, since the place name of the title—Shimadagahana, or "Shimada Point" —cannot be located. The most persuasive theory is that of Suzuki Jūzō, who argues that it is probably Shimada-chō, a block in the Fukagawa area that is completely surrounded by canals. This is given further support by a Meiji-period reference to a "Shimada Quay" (Shimadagashi) along one of the canals here (*Kadokawa Nihon chimei daijiten* 1979:351).

If this is indeed Shimada-chō, however, it seems a distorted view, for the canals of Fukagawa were calm and narrow. This looks much more like the Sumida River, which is doubtless what led Kojima Usui to propose that the mass of pilings in the foreground are the famous "Hundred Pilings" (Hyappongui) just above Ryōgoku Bridge on the east side of the Sumida (Kojima 1931:86–87). Note also the dense crowd that seems to be crossing the bridge of which we get a tiny glimpse directly above the signpost (which is marked *jōkui*, "boundary stake") to the left; no bridge or crowd of this size could have been seen from the real Shimada-chō. It is also worth noting a similarity of mood with the view of the Oumayagashi ferry in the *Thirty-six Views of Mt. Fuji*, where we look at a similar blackened form of the mountain just after the sun has set, and a similar assembly of very relaxed people. The location happens to be just around the site of the "Hundred Pilings."

I would suggest that Hokusai has made a composite view, of the sort we saw in No. 33. He has combined his close observations of waterfront life at the corner "point" (*hana*) of Shimada-chō with a broader vista of the Sumida River. It is therefore a view with a specific name, but which goes beyond any specific place to become a generic scene of evening relaxation by the water in Edo.

51. At the Foot of Fuji
(Fuji no fumoto)

Although this seems at first an innocent enough view, it is difficult to interpret. The title tells us only that we are at the foot of the mountain—never mind that the foot of the mountain is rarely as steep as this. But what are the figures up to? Four women, all in matched attire and with identical baskets on their backs, lead the group. Behind, two men carry identical pairs of baskets balanced on shoulder poles; one of them has stopped, perhaps to rest, while the other looks on with a curious expression. Behind them stands a mysterious looking figure, arms crossed in an assertive pose, a set jaw visible under the hat: he would seem to have some special authority over the group of basket-carriers. But what authority? What are the baskets for? What is going on here? There must be a hidden narrative that has yet to be discovered.

52. Fuji in a Thunderstorm
(Yūdachi no Fuji)

This immediately brings to mind "Thunderstorm Below the Mountain" in the *Thirty-six Views of Mt. Fuji*. As in No. 4, however, Hokusai has compensated for the lack of color in the book version by adding much more concrete detail, in this case a village with small figures scattering to escape the rain. We can feel the wind lashing at the thatched roofs, in contrast with the sturdy forms of the tile temple roofs to the lower right. But in the end, the overall impression is quite similar: the contrast of the sudden momentary flash of lightning over the foot of the mountain with the pure and undisturbed form of the peak above. The use of the black gradation here is particularly effective in setting off the gloom of the valley below from the white of the mountain above.

53. Fuji in the Tōtomi Mountains
(Tōtomi sanchū no Fuji)

Here again one recalls the *Thirty-six Views of Mt. Fuji*, in a print of the same name. Both views share the sense of being so high in the mountains that we feel we are actually looking down on Fuji. Tōtomi Province corresponds to the southwestern end of the present Shizuoka Prefecture, but it would be impossible to specify any particular place. In the color print version, Hokusai depicted sawyers at work on a massive square piece of timber, but here he shows us axemen at work in a tree. It is a fanciful

piece; and although it does perhaps give us a lesson in the ways that Japanese woodcutters worked, the point of the composition is in the intricate interplay of human forms, tree forms, and rope forms. A slight sense of action is provided by the bits of wood that seem to be flying from the axe of the upside-down figure to the left.

This was one of two views (with No. 35) that de Chassiron reproduced in 1861, where it was entitled "Work in the Country" (Travaux de la campagne). One suspects a certain exoticism in the implication that this is the normal appearance of Japanese at work.

54. Fuji under a Sluice
(Kakehi no Fuji)

There is no record of any wooden sluice of this description; most likely, Hokusai just dreamed it up. This is one of the few instances in which his drawing is simply not persuasive, for the water from the sluice seems to be pouring down directly on one of the boats below. The blackened form of Fuji suggests evening, and a characteristic array of figures move along the foreground slope.

55. Fuji under the Moon
(Gekka no Fuji)

If we would limit our attention to the left-hand page alone, we would have an evocative moonlight view of Fuji across a lake or river. In the middle ground, two women are beating cloth on a fulling block, a process designed to soften and bring out the sheen of cotton. It was an autumn activity of women, often envisaged as continuing on into the night in order to hasten preparations for winter, so that the image of the beaters under fall moonlight became a standard poetic and pictorial theme that had often been shown in ukiyo-e prints (as in Hokusai's own view of the poet Narihira in the *Shika shashinkyō* series of about 1834). The moon peers through the willow branches above, lighting up the women and the river below against the darkened form of Fuji.

The foreground scene to the right, however, gives an eery and almost grotesque tone to the entire composition. The large animal howling at the moon is either a dog or a wolf, although to our eyes it may not look much like either one (see *Hokusai Manga*, vol. XIV, for proof that Hokusai drew both in pretty much the same way). Particularly perplexing, however, is the stone shrine in the upper right, gleaming white in the moonlight and appearing much larger than such shrines normally were. Is there some significance to this conbination? It almost looks like something Hokusai saw in a vision or a dream.

56. Fuji the Day After Snow
(Yuki no ashita no Fuji)

In this witty composition, we discover the form of Fuji not in the mountain itself but in the mountain of snow that has been shoveled high the day after a storm. The rectangular shape of the snow shovel is echoed both in the stepped contour of the pseudo-Fuji and in the gray pattern left on the ground below. Dogs frolic on the mountain while to the right two figures, faces hidden, seem to be talking. Near them, an errand boy under a mountainously large hat makes his way through the snow with a bucket and some bottles of sake, offering a hint of warmth on a cold day.

57. Fuji of Letters
(Bunhen no Fuji)

The title has been created as an explicit counterpart to the following print, for there is no such word as *"bunhen."* The point is to suggest Fuji as the backdrop for poetic as well as military activity. The poet in question here, as Suzuki has observed, must be Yamabe Akahito, part of whose famous poem about Mt. Fuji in the *Man'yōshū* (III, 318) was eventually incorporated (with slight revisions) into the *One Hundred Poems by One Hundred Poets* (Hyakunin isshu) and thus became part of the common culture of Tokugawa Japan:

> Emerging at the shore of Tago, I see
> A robe of white:
> Snow fallen on the lofty peak of Fuji

Here the ancient poet sits, reflective, to the left, his historical distance expressed by the decorative cloudlike pattern that sets him off from the landscape beyond. It is exactly the same landscape that appears in the view of Tagonoura in the *Thirty-six Views of Mt. Fuji*, offering further confirmation of the identity of both the poet and the poem. The

activity on the beach is salt-making, for which Tagonoura was also known in poetry; similar large kiln tubs appeared in No. 25.

58. Fuji of Arms
(Buhen no Fuji)

The contrast with the previous print is, by intent, complete. "Buhen" originally meant a battle and, by extension, the practice of the military arts. A specific story is involved here, one told many times before in Tokugawa literature, art, and drama. It is the scene from the the the *Tales of the Soga* in which a great boar goes on a rampage during the hunt sponsored by the shogun Minamoto Yoritomo at the foot of Mt. Fuji. The great beast first injured several men, whom we see piled in a tangled mass to the right. Then the valiant Nitta no Shirō Tadatsune leapt on the boar's back (backwards, according to the original story—hard to tell here) and stabbed him with his short sword.

This is a particularly skillful example of Hokusai's technique of emphasizing the drama of mortal combat by the visual confusion of the struggling opponents (seen also in No. 42). In the case of Nitta and the boar, the warrior's fur leggings (*mukabaki*) make it especially difficult to distinguish man and beast: the two are as one in this decisive moment. A similar challenge in visual disentanglement is provided by the pile of men to the right; careful inspection should show four (confirmed by the number of spears).

59. Fuji Carved
(Kizami no Fuji)

Soldiers prepare to feed an army as we see Mt. Fuji "carved up" by the geometrical pattern of the bamboo fence. Suzuki suggests that this view carries over from the previous one, by depicting the meal preparation that would have been involved at such a huge hunt as the one sponsored by Yoritomo in 1193. The kind of bamboo fence here would have been the sort used in such hunts to surround the game.

In the scene, a huge cauldron of water is lodged between stones over a fire shown as stylized licks of flame. Two men seem to be lifting a large basket out of the pot; Dickins proposed that they are preparing to drain cooked rice on the bamboo rack held by the third man. Another figure to the lower left is making some sort of preparation in a low tub; perhaps this is a container for the cooked rice. A fifth figure below, immobile, serves as counterpoise to all the activity, as does Fuji above.

60. Fuji in a Window
(Sōchū no Fuji)

An old man seated at a desk stretches his arms up in an arch that echoes Fuji through the window. Western viewers since Dickins have all agreed that the gesture is one of ecstasy as he catches Fuji in a particular light, while Japanese inevitably see this as a yawn—a revealing comment on the way cultural codes of body expression differ. The Japanese perception is of course correct: simply turn the page upside down for proof.

All Japanese commentators on this print since Kojima in 1931 have emphasized the likely inspiration of Kawamura Minsetsu's view of the same title in *One Hundred Fujis* (1767). This may have provided a clue to Hokusai, but the execution is totally different. Minsetsu's image was purely architectural, with no human presence and no indication as to the size of the window; one is given the impression of a rather small one, and the view of Fuji is much more distant.

Hokusai has created a moment in time, for which the viewer must supply his own narrative. Here is mine: it is late in the day, and the poet has finally completed a difficult bit of composition. He raises his arms to stretch and yawn in satisfaction, after which he will turn to his pipe, which lies at his side. But just at the peak of his relaxation, a row of returning geese (conventional sign of the end of day) crosses the face of Fuji. As a haiku, it might be: "Stretch and yawn, encircling Fuji; returning geese."

61. Fuji in a Valley
(Tanima no Fuji)

We can make out four woodcutters: one ladling water from a spring or small waterfall in the hollow of a rock, while another pauses to change his sandals, and two more wearily make their way up from below with packs of kindling on their backs. Fuji, pure white, stands across the valley of the title.

Colophon to Volume II

The same block was used here as in Volume I, with only three small modifications. First, Hokusai's age on the first page was changed from 75 to 76, and the date on the second page was changed from Tenpō 5 to Tenpō 6 (1835). Blocks could easily be modified in this way by gouging out the area to be revised and inserting a plug (*umegi*) with the desired change.

In addition, the two characters *shohen* (Volume I) on the fold of the page have been removed. This proves that this particular impression is later than the earliest one, in which these characters were inadvertently left on the block (Forrer 1985:172).

Inside Back Cover

Framed in thick and thin bamboo is a notice, in Hokusai's own hand, for a book by himself entitled *Illustrated Album of Paitings* (Ehon nikuhitsu gachō), a set in three volumes of what appear to be instruction manuals. The separate titles, which seem to describe brush styles but defy translation, are: I. *Hanekomi usu-saishiki*; II. *Ryūsōhitsu*; III. *Jinbutsu donpitsu*. It is unclear whether this is an advertisement for a work which Hokusai actually intended to produce, or whether some sort of secret message is possibly intended, as in the titles announced in the colophon of Volumes I and II. At any rate, no such work was ever published.

Volume III

Inside Front Cover

This is a "Catalog of Picture Albums and Drawing Manuals Published by Tōhekidō of Owari," the Nagoya publisher who issued this volume. Matthi Forrer has closely studied the dating of such lists, and identifies this as Type E3, datable to the period 1850–59 (Forrer 1985:104–107, 148). This confirms that this particular impression is later than the earliest one, which has list Type D, dated 1840–47 by Forrer. See Introduction for discussion of the problems of dating Volume III.

While Minsetsu's hundred views of Mt. Fuji are orthodox, those of Hokusai are eccentric. Old Man Hokusai has taken up his vigorous brush and managed to make the peak of Fuji come to life between paper and ink, showing it from all directions, front and back, in a truly wondrous way. I have heard that he has now passed ninety years of age, and yet his sight and hearing are still like that of a youth. Perhaps he was once able to acquire the secret elixir of the Immortals on this miraculous mountain. Now the third volume has been completed, and I was asked by Gochoshi, the master of Tōhekidō, to write this preface. Having looked through the book, I record this with immense admiration.

Shippōsanka Rōjin Shōryū (Kogasa?)
[Hand-written seal]

Note: The author of this preface composed various other prefaces for Tōhekidō publications in the 1840s (see Forrer 1985:173), but nothing else is known about him; he was presumably a minor man of letters from Nagoya. The first part of the name means "Old Man at the foot of Seven-Jewel Mountain"; Shōryū ("Small Hat") is probably one of his literary names, although Forrer's reading of "Kogasa" suggests a family name.

🐦 **62.   Fuji at Akazawa**
      (Akazawa no Fuji)

Most of Hokusai's readers would have doubtless been able to identify these two wrestlers simply from the title, without looking at the names that are provided lower in the picture. Those well versed in the art of sumo would even have been able to specify the match simply from the particular tripping maneuver, by which the wrestler to the right hooks his right leg around the left calf of his opponent. It takes some imagination to predict that this will result in victory, since the hairy foe clearly has the advantage. But this is precisely the point, for this is the famous match that serves as the prologue to the *Tales of the Soga*, the tale of revenge that was so often reenacted on the stage and in the prints of Edo, in which the reigning champion of all Japan, Matano no Gorō Kunihisa (the hairy one on the left, said in the original tale to look like a fierce Guardian King) was bested by Kawazu no Saburō Sukeyasu (the white one on the right, said to look

like a gentle Boddhisatva). The move that brought victory to the underdog Kawazu is known in sumo to this day as the "Kawazu trip" (*kawazu-gake*).

The importance of this match lay more in its sequel, when Kawazu on his return from victory was felled by an arrow intended for his father. Kawazu's own two sons, Gorō and Jūrō, having taken the name of the Soga clan into which their mother remarried, resolved on a vendetta against the man responsible for their father's death. The ultimate success of this vendetta in 1193 is the central theme of the *Tales of the Soga*.

Hokusai had earlier depicted this match in *Hokusai's Drawing Style* (Hokusai gashiki) in 1819, in a view that provided a broad background landscape looking across Sagami Bay from Izu, with Mt. Fuji towering in the distance—although in fact Fuji is not visible from the present Akazawa, which is located on the east coast of the Izu Peninsula, south of Itō. Here, however, the artist has reduced the mountain almost to abstraction, in the slope to the upper right.

🐦 **63.   Fuji in the Distance from Shimotsuke Province**
      (Yashū enkei no Fuji)

The legend to the upper left of the right-hand page indicates this to be the "Priest-Crossing Pine of Mt. Nantai" (Nantaisan gyōja-goe no matsu). Suzuki Jūzō, with the help of a local historian in Tochigi Prefecture (the former Shimotsuke Province), showed that this must refer to the "Spreading Pine of Mt. Nyohō" (Nyohōzan no haimatsu) described in the *Chronicle of Nikkō* (Nikkōsan shi, 1825). This remarkable tree lay north of the peak of Mt. Nyohō, another name for the sacred Mt. Nantai at Nikkō. The pine is said to have grown in a crawling fashion, spreading out over the mountain rocks for a distance of over half a mile, crossing whole valleys. It appears that the mountain priests who came to Mt. Nantai would climb along the length of the Spreading Pine as one of their spiritual practices.

Hokusai may well have read about this pine tree in the *Chronicle of Nikkō* itself, since he is known to have provided two illustrations for the printed edition of this work, which appeared in 1837 (see Suzuki Jūzō et. al., eds. 1972:85). He then in his imagination fashioned the pine into the great arching form that we see here, placing a small shrine at the crest. Several ascetics are making their way along the snow-covered pine, one of them blowing the shell-horn of a yamabushi priest. We see Mt. Fuji from below the arch, lower in the picture than in any other view and thus imparting a sense of great loftiness to the place depicted. Mt. Nantai, lying just over one hundred miles from Mt. Fuji, ties with Fujimigahara (No. 14) as the most distant viewpoint in the *One Hundred Views of Mt. Fuji* (excepting the imaginary Orankai, No. 73).

❦ 64. Fuji in Deep Snow
(Shinsetsu no Fuji)

Travelers in a group make their way through heavy snow, which obliterates all features except for tiny slits of eyes. This is any example of a print in which the effect depends almost entirely on the gray blocks, which provide the pattern of snowflakes, the gray of the sky, and the shadow over the mountain. If it is true, as proposed in the Introduction, that the gray blocks for Volume III were designed by someone other than Hokusai, one wonders how this print might have been improved had the master himself executed it.

❦ 65. A Noble's Villa: Fuji at Sunamura
(Kika bessō Sunamura no Fuji)

Neither the title nor the place depicted has yet been figured out. Sunamura most plausibly refers to an area on the fringes of Edo, east of Fukagawa on reclaimed land along Edo Bay. But this Sunamura was known only for its Hachiman Temple, not for any "noble villa." The curious shrine shown here is dedicated to "Fudō Who Appeared from the Water." Judging from the appearance of the image inside, we may guess that a fisherman pulled out of the sea a strangely-shaped piece of rock or wood, with projections reminiscent of the flames that conventionally surround the body of the Buddhist deity Fudō. This was thought to be a miraculous find and was then enshrined in the prow of an old fishing boat as we see here.

Nagata Seiji has proposed that this is a different Sunamura, near Kisarazu in Chiba Prefecture, and has unearthed a description of a Fudō Hall there to support his argument (Nagata 1972:23). But there are Fudō halls almost anywhere in Japan, and at any rate this is not a hall; his suggestion that the reference to "from the water" refers to a much

earlier flood in the area is unconvincing. The identification of the place, particularly the sense of "a noble's villa," remains an unsolved problem. The scene is at any rate an appealing one, of men fishing for pleasure under the protection of a deity from the sea.

❦ 66. Fuji in the City
(Shichū no Fuji)

The city must be Edo, where defense against fire was a constant concern, and rooftop fire watches of this sort dotted the urban landscape. The ladders are provided with bells to sound the alarm when fire is spotted. A kite—in the shape of a *tonbi*, the bird we call a "kite"—crosses the sky, its string in perfect unison with the slope of Fuji. This view across rooftops is close in conception and composition to that of Tanabata (No. 12).

❦ 67. Fuji under Clouds
(Donten no Fuji)

In this witty conception, Fuji is shown covered by a great looming raincloud, in which we can detect the familiar shape of the mountain. The travelers in the foreground pause to prepare for the downpour; one has already donned his raincape while the other searches in a wicker hamper. The "Dōsojin" inscribed on the stone to the upper left is a god who protects wayfarers like these (comparable to the Kōshin shrine in No. 19). A composition that may be related to this view appears in *Hokusai Manga*, vol. XIX (1878). Entitled "Rain while Traveling" (Ryochū no ame), it shows two samurai very similar in attire to the ones we see here, in much the same setting, although with no Dōsojin shrine. The major difference is that the men have just completed putting on capes and hats, and the rain is already falling—hence no distant view of Fuji and no raincloud. One suspects that the *Manga* view was derived from this one.

❦ 68. Fuji and Foreign Embassy
(Raichō no Fuji)

The procession of a visiting Korean embassy moves slowly past the great mountain. Mounted on horseback to the right are two of the young boys (*kodō;*

Korean *sodong*) who were part of such processions. To the lower left, we can make out a whole band making music as they go, with two horns, two drums, a gong, and some sort of stringed instrument.

This whole conception is a revealing fantasy, by which Hokusai in effect shows a Korean embassy at two removes of the imagination. He himself had never seen an actual Korean mission to Edo, unless conceivably in 1764 at the age of five—the last time the Koreans would visit the Tokugawa capital. But every other year he had the chance to see a "Korean procession" in the form of Edo townsmen who masqueraded as a visiting embassy in the Sannō Festival parade. As Ronald Toby has argued, this "carnival of the aliens" may be seen as a symbolic way of representing "the other" in Japanese culture (Toby 1986:423). Hokusai's familiarity with the festival costume is confirmed by his depiction of part of the Korean masquerade in one vignette from his kyōka album of 1800, *Tōto meisho ichiran*. The dress and regalia of the Korean parade at the Sannō festival were closely modeled after that of the actual embassies—nine of which came to Edo between 1624 and 1764—but differed in numerous small details.

By a further displacement, the festival procession, seems to be passing by the very foot of Mt. Fuji, to which all the alien eyes are raised in awe. Hokusai thereby has subjected the Koreans to the posture of respect seen fitting from the Japanese point of view. This sense is strengthened by Hokusai's depiction of the two banners, which carry the same phrase as the title, "Raichō," literally, "coming to the [Japanese] court." This reflects the Japanese conception of such missions, that the Koreans came to pay tribute. The Koreans themselves saw it very differently, as an exchange of respect between equals, and the pennants they carried would never have borne this message.

One curious detail lies to the lower right, where three Japanese sit watching the mission in front of a notice board and what appear to be two mounds of sand—in the shape of Fuji. They suggest ritual markers, but the precise significance is unclear.

69. Fuji at Daybreak
(Akatsuki no Fuji)

Nowhere else in the series does Fuji loom so large and black as it does here, above two mail runners who make their way through the gloom just before daybreak, as the mist still lies low in the surrounding fields. The official notice board to the right, of a sort set up at frequent intervals along the Tokaido highway, carries the implication that these are runners for the shogun, carrying official documents to West Japan. They often ran in tandem like this, one carrying the mail and the other serving to clear the way. Such runners were known as *hikyaku* ("flying legs"), and by running in relay day and night, they could provide express mail service between Edo and Kyoto in three days and ten hours.

70. Fuji Straddled
(Matagi Fuji)

A cooper pounds the last stave into a large tub as Fuji appears in his crotch; we are reminded of the view of "Fujimigahara" in the *Thirty-Six Views of Mt. Fuji* in which we peer at Fuji through the tub rather than through the cooper. This kind of unexpected juxtaposition has a literary parallel in the art of haiku, as one scholar has suggested in comparing Issa's poems about Fuji and Hokusai's *One Hundred Views of Mt. Fuji* (Kuriyama 1965:85–86).

By amazing coincidence, there survives a senryū (a comic haiku) by Hokusai himself that fits this particular image almost exactly: "A strong broad stance in the shape of 'eight': summer Fuji" (Hachi no ji no funbari tsuyoshi natsu no Fuji; Iijima vol. 1, fol. 50). In Japanese, the character for "eight" resembles both the pattern of two legs spread apart and the form of Fuji's slopes. In the summer, Fuji appears clear and powerful, without the snow or clouds of winter—like a "strong stance." It is wholly plausible that this view of a cooper straddling Fuji was a direct illustration of the senryū, which is said by Iijima Kyoshin to have been composed in about 1831—just before Hokusai probably began designing the *One Hundred Views of Mt. Fuji*.

Beyond the wit, the view is also a good example of Hokusai's constant emphasis on the formal resonance between the human body and the shape of Mt. Fuji, as though man could himself incorporate the mountain (see also No. 60).

71. Fuji from Suidōbashi
(Suidōbashi Fuji)

Suidōbashi ("Aqueduct Bridge") crossed the Kanda River in Edo just west of the wooden aqueduct that carried drinking water from the Kandagawa Canal over the river and into the center of the city. The aqueduct itself, however, is not in sight in Hokusai's view, only the tiny bridge for human traffic in the distance. The manmade channel of the river here was deep and provided an appealing view of Mt. Fuji from the area of Ochanomizu that was widely depicted in ukiyo-e landscapes. Hokusai, always indifferent to topographical accuracy, shows the placid Kanda River as a swift current—and running in the wrong direction.

72. Fuji Through a Web
(Ami ni hedataru Fuji)

A decaying maple leaf is caught in a spider's web against the gray silhouette of Fuji. It is another example of a pictorial haiku, to which one of Bashō's verses seems almost perfectly matched:

Hey spider! How do you sing,   Kumo nani to
in what key?   ne o nan to naku
Wind of autumn.   aki no kaze

73. Fuji from Orankai
(Orankai no Fuji)

Hokusai's source here could have been the encyclopedia *Wakan sansai zue*, where the section on Mt. Fuji (Book 56) relates that "when Hideyoshi launched his attack against Korea, the general Katō Kiyomasa captured a prisoner in Orankai, a Japanese formerly of Matsumae by the name of Serutousu. . . . According to him, Fuji could be seen from that area on a clear day." The place "Orankai" was known in the legends surrounding Katō Kiyomasa as the farthest point to which he advanced in Korea; Suzuki quotes an 1850 account that explains the etymology of "Orankai" not as a proper name, but as a word in Korean dialect indicating any desolate and isolated place.

Suzuki argues that Hokusai therefore intends this as a depiction of Fuji seen from Korea, but the costume here is wholly different from that seen on the Koreans in No. 68. It might be noted that the word "Orankai" came to be written, as both here and in the *Wakan sansai zue*, with characters properly read "Uryanha" and originally referring to an area in Eastern Mongolia. It would seem that the term may have thus carried the sense of any strange, far-off place on the Asian continent, not necessarily

in Korea. The dress here is more reminiscent of China than Korea, as is the strangely formed stone, but it is doubtless all a product of Hokusai's imagination. The whole notion that Fuji should be visible from the Asian continent is revealing as a mark of Japan's evolving national consciousness. Wherever it is, this is the most distant point from which Fuji is depicted in the *One Hundred Views*, as Hokusai emphasizes by reducing the crater to a pointed peak.

74. Fuji in Asumi Village
(Asumimura no Fuji)

We must look twice here to find Fuji, a bare tip of white between two rooftops. The only thing in this generic village scene to help specify the location of "Asumi Village" is the sense, from the position of Fuji, that we are high in the mountains. The only candidate for an actual place, Suzuki reports, is an Asumi in Yamanashi Prefecture. The map reveals, however, that this is located close by Yoshida, at the very base of Mt. Fuji, from which this view is inconceivable; it is also written with different characters. Wherever it may be, the tiny tip of Fuji between the rooftops of a Japanese village is a witty and touching sight.

75. Fuji from the Sumida River
(Sumida no Fuji)

The title, the flowering cherry trees, and the groups of people relaxing here and there tell us that this must be the area east of the Sumida River in Edo known as Mukōjima, famed for its spring blossoms. Somehow it is not a particularly appealing scene. The cherry trees, to begin with, are unimpressive; the rather scrawny form is no different from those in the view of Gotenyama in the *Thirty-Six Views of Mt. Fuji*, to be sure, but there is no compensation for the absence of color in the clumsy design and execution of the gray blossoms here (in striking contrast to No. 29). The terrain here is also more rough and hilly than the level, low-lying area of Mukōjima itself, and most peculiar of all, none of the figures show any facial features. I sense a certain perversity in this strange variant of an area that had been depicted in such a pleasant way so many times before in ukiyo-e prints.

76. Circling the Crater of Fuji
(Hakkai-meguri no Fuji)

In the Fujikō religion today, the practice of circling the crater of Mt. Fuji after reaching the top is known as Ohachimawari ("going around the sacred bowl"). In the title of Hokusai's view here, the rim around the crater is referred to as the "Eight Worlds," an image that dates back to the medieval period when, under the influence of esoteric Buddhism, the summit of Fuji came to be conceived of as an eight-petaled lotus blossom. Accordingly, eight separate peaks were distinguished, and the names of Buddhist deities assigned to each.

Here Hokusai shows the progress of pilgrims around the crater, the black depths of which we see in the center; in the pamphlet handed out today at the shrine at the summit, the crater is known as the "Inner Temple" (Naiin) or "Shrine of Mystery" (Yūgū). The pilgrims here climb up and down in a sweeping arch, over a rock face that is so steep they must shed their caps (and apparently climbing sticks), which are left in the care of one of the climbers in a stack on a rock below to the right. On descending to the left, the caps are waiting to the picked up again (leaving us to wonder how they got from one place to the other).

The actual rim of Fuji is not quite so mountainous as here envisioned by Hokusai, who surely never saw it in person, but there are spots, near the peaks of Kengamine or Hakusandake, which are every bit as scary.

77. Fuji of Elegant Delight
(Fuzei omoshiroki Fuji)

This is undoubtedly the most complex exercise of visual wit in the entire series, in what I would interpret as a visual form of linked verse (renga). The basic principle of renga is that different poets in sequence take up the concluding section of a previous verse and use it as the first section of a new one.

The first verse would be the foreground, where we see a group of three men: one older above, one middle-aged on the ground, and one younger in between; their shaved heads and attire suggest traveling renga poets. The raised embankment seems to be the entrance to a temple, where perhaps they have just attended a renga party. One of the three

has somehow slipped down to the ground; some earth seems to have spilled out from between the stones of the wall at the same time. He is not hurt, and his companions join in laughter at the slipup.

The man on the ground links to a second image because of the way his leg seems to be kicking upward: it looks as though he has kicked up a ball, which flies high into the air. The ball in question, with its stitched seam, is a "kickball" (kemari), and the game of keeping it in the air had first emerged among aristocrats of the Heian court; as is required for the present link, it had in fact become more popular by the Tokugawa period.

In the final link, the kicked-up ball then strikes an accidental pose against the tip of Fuji, as though it were the moon rising beyond the mountain (although in a further comic twist, it can also be seen as a giant snowball rolling earthward, for this appears to be a winter scene). The image of the moon rising over Fuji ends on a serious poetic image that has been reached by comic links. Hence the "elegant delight" of the title.

78. The Farmhand of Fuji in Kai Province
(Kai no Fuji nō-otoko)

The "Farmhand" is the figure that we see in black on the face of Mt. Fuji, or is it possibly a farmhand couple—a man with a hoe on the left and a woman on the right? The tradition, at any rate, was that in the spring of certain years, as the mountain snow melted, there would appear on the upper slopes of Fuji the form of a farmhand (nō-otoko), and that this was a sign that the crops would be plentiful. This folklore can apparently be found for various mountains in Japan, although the case of Fuji generally refers to the view from Tagonoura, to the south. In his title, however, Hokusai places it on the opposite side.

Below is a scene that perfectly complements the auspicious sign above, as two farmhands—the arching arm and back of the one on the right a perfect image of the form of Fuji above—haul bags of rice seed from a soaking pond. The seed will then be planted in the beds beyond, net-covered to keep off hungry birds, and finally transplanted as seedlings into paddies that will grow to produce the bounteous crop promised by the Farmhand of Fuji.

❦ 79. Summer Fuji in Inage-ryō
(Inage-ryō natsu no Fuji)

In the center, long strips of cloth are laid out after being rinsed in the water of the river nearby. On the near shore, we can make out the heads of three people who seem to be making their way along the edge of the water. All three carry bolts of cloth, packed in the woman's basket and laid over the pole shouldered by two men; presumably they are about to rinse them in the stream. On the embankment above, in the right foreground, three men and three woman have taken a meal break, eating from lunch boxes and heating tea over a fire.

Fuji above appears in solid black, lined by white clouds. In most instances in this series, a black Fuji indicates nighttime—whether just after sunset (No. 50), or under moonlight (No. 55), or before daybreak (No. 69). Here, however, it would seem to emphasize that this is summer, when all the snow has melted and the sun burns down hot upon the mountain; note that this is the only title in the entire series in which the season is specified. The title here also specifies a place, Inage-ryō, an area that lies just south of the Tama River, in what is now Kanagawa Prefecture, across from the present Futako-Tamagawa. It is plausible that the river shown here is the Tama, which was associated with the washing and fulling of cloth. The place, however, was not at all well known, and Hokusai must have had some personal reason for specifying it.

❦ 80. Fuji at Torigoe
(Torigoe no Fuji)

Torigoe was the area of Edo, north of the Asakusa Gate, where the Calendar Bureau of the shogunate was located. Here an observatory was built, for this was the official center for the study of astronomy, which was increasingly influenced by Western knowledge in the late Tokugawa period. The great spherical apparatus that Hokusai has shown here is not in fact intended for observation and hence would surely not be found on the rooftop of the observatory. It is known as an orrery, after the Earl of Orrery who sponsored its invention in England in the early eighteenth century, and is a mechanical model of the solar system, intended to demonstrate the periods of the planets.

It is highly unlikely that Hokusai had ever seen an orrery. More likely he encountered an illustra-

tion of one in the writings of Shiba Kōkan. In one of the ten etchings in his *Complete Illustrations of the Heavens* (Tenkyū zenzu, 1796), for example, Kōkan shows an elaborate orrery (illustrated in French 1974:137), which one judges from the zodiacal figures to have been made in Japan. Hokusai's orrery looks nothing like Kōkan's, however, for it lacks the critical components of the sun and planets that were so important to Kōkan, who prized the device as tangible demonstration that the sun is the center of the universe. A real orrery, moreover, sat on a table, not on a roof. We can take Hokusai's device rather as an emblem of his fascination with Western science and of his own preoccupation with regularities of geometrical form.

❦ 81. Fuji over a Waterfall
(Takigoshi no Fuji)

In a homely family vignette, a woodcutter carries the kindling and the baby while his wife carries the axe and a basket of leaves. To the right, we are reminded of the highly abstract and decorative forms assumed by waterfalls in the series *Touring the Waterfalls in the Various Provinces* (Shokoku taki meguri, c. 1833), which Hokusai had done shortly before. Here, the result is not a great success.

❦ 82. Fuji at a Village Boundary
(Murazakai no Fuji)

Boundaries in traditional Japan were marked with shrines and devices to propitiate the gods who dwelled there. The marker in this case is a curious one, consisting of the familiar strips of folded paper (*gohei*) and stretch of twisted rope, but arranged in such a way that a rock tied below serves to weight the pole of *gohei* in an upright position. Perhaps Hokusai had seen such a marker on his travels, or perhaps he devised it as a way of creating a reflected form of Fuji in the shape of the rope. Below, an assortment of humanity of the sort one might expect passing between villages.

❦ 83. Fuji at Aoyama
(Aoyama no Fuji)

An umbrella maker applies waterproofing oil to an assembled umbrella in the midst of a playful display of forms, the cones of the folded umbrellas appearing as a range of lesser peaks below Fuji, and the open ones as clouds passing overhead. The Aoyama of the title presumably refers to the Edo district of that name, but the connection with the umbrella making is obscure. The markings on the umbrellas are "Bookstore" (*shoshi*), to the left, and the title of this series (*Fugaku hyakkei*), beyond. It was not unusual to include self-advertising in pictures in this manner, although the information about the publisher is curiously vague. More such information appears four views later.

84. Fuji behind a Net
(Amiura no Fuji)

A fisherman heaves back, one foot propped on the gunwale, to hoist his "four-handed net" (*yotsude-ami*) from the river, and through it we see the form of Fuji etched along the weave. It is a witty conception, delicately executed.

85. Fuji under a Bridge
(Kyōka no Fuji)

It has been proposed by various scholars that the conception of viewing Fuji under a bridge may be traced back to one of Kawamura Minsetsu's *Hundred Fujis* of 1767. Although there is no way to prove this influence, Hokusai clearly liked the idea, for it appears in one of his early Western-style landscapes, then in "Mannenbashi" in the *Thirty-Six Views of Mt. Fuji*, and earlier in this series in No. 48. All such earlier views, however, involved ordinary arched wooden bridges, while here we see a very curious flat bridge that seems to be supported by the sawed-off branches of an old tree. This arrangement seems too particular to be a product of Hokusai's imagination, but no record has yet been found of any such bridge.

86. Fuji with a Scaffold
(Ashiro no Fuji)

Two masons are plastering a storehouse, presumably in Edo, in a complex geometry of the rectilinear scaffolding and the curved forms of the bodies. One man shovels up the mortar that he has mixed below,

while the other applies it with his trowel, leaving the pattern of undried gray on the wall above. This depiction of the rhythms of reciprocal labor recalls the view of workmen stacking lumber in "Honjo Tatekawa," or tossing bundles of tile in "Suruga-chō," in the *Thirty-Six Views of Mt. Fuji*.

87. Fuji in a Downpour
(Murasame no Fuji)

The "*murasame*" of the title literally means "rain in a cluster" and refers to a sudden, heavy downpour of the sort that Hokusai has nicely conveyed here. The contour of the mountain appearing through the rain is outlined by the use of the gray block alone, heightening the sense of abstraction that allows one to see the mountain in the rain (an impossibility).

The umbrella on the right bears the characters "Volume Three" and is perhaps related to those with similar information in No. 83. Hokusai may be wittily suggesting that one of the umbrellas manufactured earlier in Aoyama is now being put to the test in a real rain. More likely, there is some clue here concerning the puzzling circumstances of the publication of Volume III.

88. Fuji with a Rocket
(Rōen [noroshi] no Fuji)

The rocket of the title appears as a small eel-like creature high in the sky above Fuji. This is not the sort of rocket designed for visual pleasure and set off above the Sumida River during summer evenings in Edo, but rather a signal rocket for military use. Maneuvers with such rockets were held near the mouth of the Sumida every year in late summer, sponsored by the bakufu. This is presumably what is illustrated here, and Suzuki has suggested that the houses to the left and below represent the tiny fishermen's island of Tsukudajima. This is supported by the view below of fishermen charring the bottom of their boat with pine torches (to prevent rotting) and in the black peaks of drying nets (mini-Fuji forms that recall those of No. 68) to the lower right and upper left. If this is in fact Tsukudajima, however, Hokusai has turned the low seawalls into steep cliffs at the left, and few would recognize the place.

89. Fukurokuju
(Fukurokuju)

This decorative view, as Suzuki has pointed out, is a rebus for "Fukurokuju," the name of one of the Seven Gods of Happiness. *Fuku* and *-roku-*, both of which mean "good luck," are represented as animals, which are homonyms when read in the Chinese manner: *fuku* for bat and *roku* for deer. Hence we see the deer on the rock below and the three bats in the sky. Mt. Fuji itself then becomes *-ju*, "longevity," a token of the old tradition of Fuji as a source of the elixir of immortality.

According to information in Williams (1976:34,116), the Chinese themselves used the bat and deer as rebuses, but with slightly different characters (although these would also be possible): the bat (*pien fu*) was used to represent "wealth" (*fu*), and the deer (*lu*) as a sign for an official emolument (*lu*). The latter character is in fact precisely the one that appears in the title here; Suzuki claimed this must be an error, but it seems more likely taken directly from Chinese practice.

The symbolism of immortality is carried through in the very person of Fukurokuju, the god of immortality, and in his companion, the deer, who is reported in Chinese legend to be "a long-lived creature; but instead of becoming white in its old age, it changes to blue when a thousand years old, and to black at its second millenium" (Joly 1967:154). The whole view thus takes on a highly auspicious quality and may be interpreted in particular as a reflection of Hokusai's obsession with ever longer life.

90. Fuji from the Bucket-Ferry on the Ōi River
(Ōigawa okegoe no Fuji)

There really was a place on the upper reaches of the Ōi River, it appears, where large tubs like this one were used for crossing because of the prohibition of both bridges and boat ferries as a measure of military security. Here we see the two boatmen, in rhythm with the form of Fuji, each using a long pole and standing on a board lashed on to the rim. In the tub below huddle four (or more?) passengers, enduring what cannot have been a very pleasant experience. Suzuki reports that the bucket-ferries on the Ōi River survived until late Meiji.

91. Fuji through a Partition
(Mikiri no Fuji)

A painter is putting the finishing touches on a newly completed shop engaged in the business of renting out boats. The sign above, written in Hokusai's distinctive hand, advertises the variety of craft available: covered pleasure boats for a large group (*yanebune*), small cargo boats (*nitari*), fast taxi-boats for two or three passengers (*chokibune*), and fishing boats (*tsuribune*). The variety listed here would only have been available in Edo, on the Sumida River, which we see beyond. Below, the painter completes his task by inscribing a lantern that will stand before the shop. The slogan to the side expresses hope for a steady succession of loyal patrons (*senkyaku banrai*, "one thousand customers, ten thousand visits"), and the word just completed is the name of the shop—sure enough, the Fuji-ya.

Resting beside a post is a shoji screen to be used as a partition in the new shop, and we see Fuji through the rectangular grid of the lattice. It is unusual for a shoji; they normally have a wood panel along the bottom for protection, a section of solid paper above that, and then the wooden lattice covered with translucent paper to admit light. Even if it is upside down here, it should have a panel rather than lattice at the top. Hokusai was taking his usual liberties.

The title here perplexed Suzuki Jūzō when writing in 1972, since *mikiri* usually means "to sell cheaply." Since then, however, the dictionary *Nihon kokugo daijiten* (1972–76) has appeared and reports that *mikiri* does sometimes have the sense, true to the literal meaning "vision cut off," of a partition, giving examples of a standing screen or a wall. It is less clear whether it would normally apply to a shoji, which admits light, but it was surely this usage that inspired the title here.

92. Fuji from the Musashi Plain
(Musashino no Fuji)

This is Hokusai's version of an ancient poetic conception of the Musashi Plain, the broad upland area west of Edo, as a place covered with deep grass. To this in time was added the image of the moon over the grassy plain, as in the poem: "The plain of Musashi: no mountains for the moon to enter; it rises from the grasses, sinks back into the grass"

(Smith 1986a:22). It must be recalled that in most of Japan, particularly in the traditional capital area of Nara and Kyoto, the moon always set behind mountains, so that the idea of moon seen through low grasses was a novel one. Hokusai, however, was of course obliged to show the moon setting behind his one special mountain, a combination that did in fact often appear on a genre of decorative screens depicting the Musashi Plain (Musashino zu byōbu). The stylized bands of clouds here are suggestive of traditional painting in the Yamato-e style and emphasize the classical nature of the theme.

93. Fuji in a Grass Hoop
(Chinowa no Fuji)

Summer in traditional Japan was considered a time of danger from sickness and heat, so a variety of means were devised to ward off the evil spirits, one of which we see here. A kind of grass known as *chigaya*, a member of the rice family and a plant with medicinal uses that may have recommended it for the purpose, was twisted and bound to form a large hoop, and then hung as we see here from a wooden torii within the precincts of a shrine; here a Shintō priest is blessing the *chinowa* ("hoop of *chigaya*") with a wand of paper gohei. On the evening before the first day of the Sixth Month, a ceremony of purification was held, and those passing through the loop were purged of the baleful effects of summer miasma.

To the lower left is the strange sight of a tree from which water flows into a stone enclosure below. A similar tree is depicted by Hokusai in the *Manga*, vol. XIV (c. 1850s) with the title "Water-Giving Tree" (Suishōboku), which shows a man drinking the water from a cup. One suspects that the phenomenon occurred in more places than one; but I believe that the view here can be precisely located within the precincts of the Takada Inari Shrine in Edo, where the *Edo meisho zue* (Book IV) reports that "In the Fourth Month of Genroku 15 [1702], there was a sign from the gods and a sacred spring gushed forth from the hollow of a hackberry tree (*enoki*). When those suffering from diseases of the eye wash in this water, miracles occur." In the view here, the man to the left seems clearly to be placing the water over his eyes. The actual tree, from which water did indeed flow, survived until destroyed in a bombing

raid during the Pacific War. The shrine has been moved to a different location but remains in the Takada area around Waseda University.

94. Surprise-View Fuji
(Futomiru Fuji)

The view of Fuji itself through the old crumbling tile wall does not strike us, or apparently the men below, as that surprising. Perhaps the point is in the juxtaposition of the old wall covered with snow and the fresh flowers and shoots beyond. Suzuki interprets these as autumn grasses, but I think that spring makes more sense, both because of the snow and because of the appropriate symbolism of Fuji as new life rising from old ruins.

95. Fuji with Broken Form in Deep Mountain Mist
(Sanki fukaku katachi o kuzusu no Fuji)

In the foreground are two figures so gracefully poised one against the other than it is difficult to think of them as rough men of the mountain. Each has his identifying tool: an axe for the woodcutter on the left and a gun for the hunter on the right. The woodcutter turns his pipe upside down to borrow a light from the hunter, and in the shape of the joined pipes we see Fuji itself turned over: we can even imagine the flame passed from one to the other as the crater of the volcano. The darkened form of Fuji shows that evening is falling, as the mountain mists of the title gather in the valleys below and work their way up the face of Fuji beyond, slowly "breaking down its form" as the darkness settles.

96. Fuji with a Cuckoo
(Kakkō no Fuji)

A stylish older gentleman sits on some sort of platform (for moon-viewing? a boat-landing?) looking out over a river and marshes beyond. In the sky, a cuckoo wings across the face of the mountain, a sign of early summer. (The bird in question must be the *hototogisu*, a small cuckoo often depicted like this, and not the large *kakkō* of the title, a bird that rarely shows itself.) The long robe and outsized fan held by the gentleman suggest a certain affectation for things Chinese of a sort that Hokusai often betrayed in his own art.

97. Fuji from Rakanji Temple
(Rakanji no Fuji)

Only the tip of the temple indicated in the title appears here—an elaborate rooftop ornament of the sort commonly found on Buddhist pagodas, with rings indicating the nine heavens of the Buddhist universe, and culminating in symbolic flames at the top. There was no pagoda, however, in the precincts of Rakanji temple, which lay on the eastern edge of Edo, but it did have two other very unusual structures. One was a huge hall that housed over five hundred wooden statues representing disciples of the Buddha (*rakan*). The building that Hokusai has shown us, however, was the better known: a three-floor structure with a spiral circuit inside that took one upwards through a symbolic "pilgrimage" of images representing one hundred Kannon temples throughout Japan, and finally out onto a viewing platform at the top. Hokusai had shown a view of Fuji from this platform in the *Thirty-Six Views of Mt. Fuji*, with an intermediate landscape of which we see a compressed version here. To the far right are the tall poles representing the lumber yards along the Tatekawa Canal, with broad marshy fields between (which look more like a large pond in the earlier view).

As noted by Suzuki, the roof ornament on the Spiral Hall which is shown in the *Edo meisho zue* (vol. VII, 1836), is much simpler than the one shown here. Earlier views, however, such as that in Kitao Masayoshi's *Ehon Azuma kagami* (1787), show a considerably more elaborate ornament, if not of the complexity of Hokusai's, and may reflect an earlier version with which Hokusai was familiar. Hokusai himself, however, had in fact drawn a detailed view of the building many years earlier (illustrated in Narazaki 1943:fig. 122), which shows an ornament that would fall in complexity somewhere between that of Masayoshi and the one we see here; there is no doubt that Hokusai was given to elaboration.

One other detail in Masayoshi's view may be relevant, for it shows a large crane's nest perched on the roof of the Rakan Hall. This would be just the direction in which the row of descending storks in Hokusai's view are heading.

98. Fuji from Senzoku
(Senzoku no Fuji)

The title must refer to Senzoku Pond, which lay in a hilly area some seven miles southeast of central Edo. In the gazetteer *Edo meisho zue* (III, 1834), the main attraction of the pond is an old pine tree on which the priest Nichiren is said to have hung his robe. Hokusai's choice of place here may have somehow been related to his own Nichiren faith, but he shows us nothing of the pine tree nor in fact anything distinctive—simply a pond vaguely outlined in gray, and a few ordinary travelers making their way south.

99. Fuji through a Knothole
(Fushiana no Fuji)

In a picture reminiscent of No. 44, a servant engaged in cleaning pauses to point out a striking optical illusion to some guests, who stretch their fingers in contorted gestures of amazement; the figure below is in fact strikingly similar in pose to that in "The First Hanging Scroll." Here the illusion involves the pinhole effect, essentially the principle of a camera, by which a tiny hole will act as a convex lens to project an inverted image on a surface. In this instance, the image of Fuji passes through a knothole in the protective shutters (which are still closed, so the time must be early morning, when the rising sun is bright on the mountain), and is then cast on the translucent paper of the shoji across the hallway.

Suzuki has assembled an intriguing variety of evidence, primarily from the writings of the novelist Takizawa Bakin, to show that this phenomenon had been observed from time to time in late Tokugawa Japan, apparently always through knotholes in wood panels. Bakin describes in detail his awe at the astonishing detail of the images, and at the fact that they were in color. Neither Bakin nor anyone else ever appears to have sought a logical explanation for these strange images, which were seen as inexplicable and peculiar to certain places. Hokusai may well have heard of the phenomenon from Bakin, for whom he had illustrated many novels, or he may have observed it himself somewhere.

The one inexplicable detail in Hokusai's own depiction is the outline of a second Fuji in the image cast on the shoji. Suzuki suggests that he is distinguishing between an "actual image" (*jitsuzō*) and an "illusion" (*kyozō*), but this seems too philosophical for Hokusai. It remains a mystery to me, as any such image was a mystery to Hokusai.

100. Fuji from the Seashore
(Kaihin no Fuji)

The place is not specified, and no such overhanging rock form of note has been discovered in the area around Fuji. Hokusai had, however, shown rather similar formations in earlier landscapes, as for example in an illustration of Matsushima in *Hinaura tsuki kuwashi* of 1803 (Hillier 1980:54). A more likely candidate for the actual place is depicted in a block drawing *(hanshita-e)* illustrated in Narasaki (1943:380), which shows a very similar rock formation. The location is described as Mt. Nokogiri, on the Chiba Peninsula, which would offer just the sort of view across water that we see here, with a lovely pattern of seaweed on the beach below and an abstract pattern of water in between. At best, however, the other view was only a hint, for the rock has here been placed much closer to the shore.

101. Fuji from Snake-Chasing Swamp
(Jaoinuma no Fuji)

Jaoinuma (or Hebioinuma), "Snake-Chasing Swamp," is presumably a proper name, but no such place has ever been found. It is clearly a swamp of sorts, and to the left a curious open structure lies near the water—perhaps a platform for entertainment or moon-viewing. The image of Mt. Fuji on the water appears reflected, enlarged, and asymmetrical—an optical impossibility, but a conception that clearly appealed to Hokusai. A variant of the idea appears in the striking view in the *Thirty-Six Views of Mt. Fuji* in which the rough summer form of Fuji is reflected on the surface of Lake Kawaguchi as a snowcapped winter peak.

102. Fuji Concluded in One Stroke
(Taibi ippitsu no Fuji)

Try to follow the course of the single stroke that brings the series to a close, as it begins in a puddle of ink below, creeping its way up in a ragged pattern left and occasionally right, increasingly refined, then pulling free from the clouds to taper upward to the peak of Fuji, there jabbing in the crater and descending in a finale to the right. "One-stroke painting" was a standard trick in the repertoire of the Edo painter, and one at which Hokusai was particularly skilled; it is no surprise that he should indulge in such a mark of virtuosity.

Yet there is also a concluding fullness in the parallel with the contours of Hokusai's life, which began with long years of apprenticeship and practice in the lower ranks of the world of ukiyo-e, was marked by muddling progress upwards, upwards to the fine book illustrations of the 1820s and the great landscapes of the early 1830s, crested, it must be said in retrospect, with the *One Hundred Views of Mt. Fuji* itself, and then descended down, yet strongly, to his exit at age ninety. Hokusai himself must have known that even as he drew the peak where the elixir of the Immortals lay, the form of the mountain itself dictated a final descent.

103. Inside Back Cover

This page bears an advertisement for two publications by Tōhekidō, one a manual on tea preparation (*Sencha hayashinan*) and one an album of haiku (*Haikai goshichi shū*). This is advertisement Type 40 in Forrer's scheme, but sheds no further light on dating (Forrer 1985:122). At the end of the page is the publisher's name, Eirakuya Tōshirō, with the addresses of the main store in Nagoya (Honchō-dōri 7-chōme) and a branch in Edo (Nihonbashi-dōri at Hon-Shirogane-chō 2-chōme).

ðŸ•® Bibliography ðŸ•®

In addition to authors and works cited in the introduction and commentaries, other important works of direct bearing on the *One Hundred Views of Mt. Fuji* are included in this bibliography. In the instance of premodern works, the most useful and/or accessible modern edition is cited. For a full bibliography on Hokusai, see Suzuki, et al. eds. (1972). Place of publication for Japanese books is Tokyo.

de Bary, Wm. Theodore, eds. et al. *Sources of Chinese Tradition*. New York: Columbia University Press, 1960.

de Chassiron, Charles. *Notes sur le Japon, la Chine, et l'Inde*. Paris: Dentu and Reinwald, 1861.

Dickins, Frederick V. *Fugaku Hiyaku-kei: One Hundred Views of Fuji (Fusiyama) by Hokusai*. London: Batsford, 1880. Reprinted by Frederick Publications (New York, 1958) without the preface and with a new introduction by Jack Hillier, together with photographic reproductions of the original Hokusai prints, most of them in mirror image.

Edo meisho zue (1834–36): Suzuki Tōzō and Asakura Haruhiko, eds., *Shinpan Edo meisho zue*. 3 vols. Kadokawa shoten, 1974.

Forrer, Matthi. *Eirakuya Tōshirō, Publisher at Nagoya—A Contribution to the History of Publishing in 19th Century Japan*. Japonica Neerlandica, Monographs of the Netherlands Association for Japanese Studies, Vol. 1. Amsterdam: J.C. Gieben, 1985.

Freed, Stanley A., and Freed, Ruth S. "Swastika: A New Symbolic Interpretation." *Rice University Studies* 66 (1980):87–105.

French, Calvin L. *Shiba Kōkan: Artist, Innovator, and Pioneer in the Westernization of Japan*. New York and Tokyo: Weatherhill, 1974.

Fujisan ki (c. 887): *Gunsho ruijū*, IX (kan 135).

de Goncourt, Edmond. *Hokousai*. Paris: Bibliothèque Charpentier, 1896.

Harigaya, Shōkichi, eds. et al. *Ukiyo-e bunken mokuroku*. Mitō shooku, 1972.

Hillier, Jack. *Hokusai: Paintings, Drawings and Woodcuts*. 3d ed. London: Phaidon Press, 1978.

————. *The Art of Hokusai in Book Illustration*. London: Sotheby Parke Bernet; Berkeley and Los Angeles: University of California Press, 1980.

————. *The Art of the Japanese Book*. 2 vols. London: Philip Wilson/Sotheby's Publications, 1987.

Hokusai Manga (15 vols, 1814–78): reproduced in 3 vols. Iwasaki Bijutsusha, 1986–87. Compiled, with commentaries, by Nagata Seiji.

Iijima, Hanjirō (Kyoshin). *Katsushika Hokusai den*. 2 vols. Hōsūkaku, 1893.

Inobe, Shigeo. *Fuji no shinkō*. Meicho shuppan, 1983. Originally published as [Kanpei taisha] Sengen jinja shamusho, ed., *Fuji no kenkyū, 2* (Kokin shoin, 1929).

Ishigami, Katashi. *Nihon minzokugo daijiten*. Ōfūsha, 1985.

Iso, Hiroshi. "Kawamura Minsetsu no 'Hyaku Fuji' to Hokusai no Fugaku zu." *Bigaku ronkyū* 1 (1961):67–84.

Joly, Henri L. *Legend in Japanese Art*. Rutland, Vermont and Tokyo: Charles E. Tuttle, 1967. Originally published in 1908 by John Lane, London.

Kadokawa Nihon chimei daijiten, 13: Tokyo-to. Kadokawa shoten, 1979.

Kawakita, Michiaki. *Fugaku hyakkei*. Includes English text "Hokusai's *One Hundred Views of Mt. Fuji*." Unsōdō, 1965. Published with a woodblock facsimile edition of the *One Hundred Views of Mt. Fuji*.

Keene, Donald, trans. "The Tale of the Bamboo Cutter." *Monumenta Nipponica* 11 (1955): 329–55.

Kobayashi, Tadashi. "Sōsetsu: Fugaku Sanjūrokkei" and "Zuhan kaisetsu." In Zauhō kankōkai, ed., *Fugaku Sanjūrokkei*, Ukiyo-e taikei, 13 (Shūeisha, 1976), pp. 58–64, 105–123.

Kojiki: Donald L. Philippi, trans. Princeton, N.J.: Princeton University Press; Tokyo: University of Tokyo Press, 1969.

Kojima, Usui. *Edo makki no ukiyo-e*. Azusa shobō, 1931.

Kokusho sōmokuroku. 9 vols. Iwanami shoten, 1963–76.

Kondō, Ichitarō. *The Thirty-Six Views of Mount Fuji by Hokusai*. Honolulu: East-West Center Press, 1966.

Kuriyama, Riichi. "Tōsaku to nejire." *Kokubungaku: Kaishaku to kanshō* 30.6 (May 1965):79-86.

Manga: see *Hokusai Manga*.

Matsuda, Teizō, [*Shintō Shingon*] *Myōjutsu hihō taizen*. 6th ed. Jingūkan, 1969.

Nagata, Seiji. *Katsushika Hokusai nenpu*. Sansai shinsha, 1985.

―――. "Hiroshige shinshutsu-go no Hokusai." *Ukiyo-e geijutsu* 30 (1971):24-26.

―――. "Bōsō no ryokaku Katsushika Hokusai." *Ukiyo-e geijutsu* 35 (1972):20-26.

―――, ed. *Hokusai no edehon*. 5 vols. Iwasaki bijutsusha, 1986.

Nakamura, Kyoko Motomochi. *Miraculous Stories from the Japanese Buddhist Tradition: The Nihon Ryōiki of the Monk Kyōkai*. Cambridge: Harvard University Press, 1973.

Narazaki, Muneshige. *Hokusai ron*. Atorie-sha, 1944.

―――. *Fugaku sanjūrokkei*. Hokusai to Hiroshige, 1. Kōdansha, 1971.

―――, et. al. *Hokusai*. Nikuhitsu ukiyo-e, 7. Shūeisha, 1982.

Naruse, Fujio. "Nihon kaiga ni okeru Fuji-zu no teikeiteki hyōgen ni tsuite," *Bijutsushi* 112 (1982):115-30.

Nippon Gakujutsu Shinkōkai, comp. *The Man'yōshū*. New York: Columbia University Press, 1965.

Nishiyama, Matsunosuke. "Edokko." In *Edo chōnin no kenkyū*, ed., Nishiyama Matsunosuke, 2. Yoshikawa kōbunkan, 1973: 1-93.

Oda, Kazuma. *Hokusai*. Arusu, 1926.

Ogawa, Takanori. "Fujisan no chishitsu―Utsukushii san'yō no himitsu." In Asahi shinbunsha, ed., *Fujisan zennanai* (Asahi shinbunsha, 1985), pp. 64-67.

Sawada, Akira. "Fuji no bijutsu." In [Kanpei taisha] Sengen jinja shamusho, ed., *Fuji no kenkyū*, 4 (Kokin shoin, 1929): 1-169.

Smith, Henry D., II. "Sky and Water: The Deep Structures of Tokyo." In *Tokyo: Form and Spirit*, ed., Mildred Friedman. Minneapolis: Walker Art Center; New York: Abrams, 1986:20-35.

―――. *Hiroshige: One Hundred Famous Views of Edo*. New York: George Braziller, 1986.

Sorimachi, Shigeo. *Catalogue of Japanese Illustrated Books and Manuscripts in the Spencer Collection of the New York Public Library*. Kōbunsō, 1978.

Starr, Frederick. *Fujiyama―The Sacred Mountain of Japan*. Chicago: Covici-McGee, 1924.

Suzuki, Jūzō. *Ningen Hokusai*. Genshoku-ban ukiyo-e bunko, 3. Ryokuen shobō, 1963.

―――. *Fugaku hyakkei kaisetsu*. Iwasaki Bijutsusha, 1972. Published with facsimile reproduction of *One Hundred Views of Mt. Fuji*. Revised slightly for one-volume edition: *Katsushika Hokusai Fugaku hyakkei* (Iwasaki Bijutsusha, 1986). The general essay from the 1972 edition (but not the commentaries on the individual views) also appears as "Fugaku hyakkei" in Suzuki Jūzō, *Ehon to ukiyo-e* (Bijutsu shuppansha, 1979): 303-329.

―――, et al. eds. *Zaigai hihō: Hokusai*. Gakushū kenkyūsha, 1972.

Takayanagi, Mitsutoshi. "Fuji no bungaku." In [Kanpei taisha] Sengen jinja shamusho, ed., *Fuji no kenkyū*, vol. 4. Kokin shoin, 1929:1-282.

Takeda, Hisayoshi, ed. *Fujisan*. Nihon chiri taikei, supp. vol. 5. Kaizōsha, 1931.

Takeshima, Hagoromo. "Uta ni arawaretaru Fujisan." *Rekishi chiri* 36.1 (July 1920): 5-14.

Takeuchi, Melinda. "Ike Taiga: A Biographical Study." *Harvard Journal of Asiatic Studies* 43 (1983):141-86.

Toby, Ronald. "Carnival of the Aliens―Korean Embassies in Edo-Period Art and Popular Culture." *Monumenta Nipponica* 41 (1986): 415-456.

Tōgasaki, Fumiko. "Hokusai sakuhin ni okeru kihonteki kōzu ni tsuite: Mitsuwari no hō to kiku hōen no hō" (Certain aspects of the basic compositional elements in Hokusai's work: "The Law of the Three Divisions" and "The Method of Ruler and Compass"). *Ukiyo-e geijutsu* 51(1976):3-27 (English summary, i–v) and 52 (1976):14-26.

Tsuji, Nobuo. *Hokusai*. Bukku obu bukkusu Nihon no bijutsu, 31. Shōgakkan, 1982.

Tyler, Royall. "A Glimpse of Mt. Fuji in Legend and Cult." *Journal of the Association of Teachers of Japanese* 16(1981):140-65.

Wakan sansai zue (1712), comp. Terashima Ryōan. 2 vols. Nihon zuihitsu taisei kankōkai, 1929.

Ware, James R., trans. *The Sayings of Mencius*. Mentor Books, 1960.

Williams, C. A. S. *Outlines of Chinese Symbolism and Art Motives*. 3d. rev. ed. 1941. Reprint. New York: Dover Publications, 1976.

Yasuda, Gōzō. *Gakyō Hokusai*. Yūkō shobō, 1971.

Yoshida, Teruji, *Ukiyo-e jiten*. 3 vols. 3d ed. Gabundō, 1974.